The Last of the Old-Time Cowboys

Patrick Dearen

Republic of Texas Press

Library of Congress Cataloging in Publication Data

Dearen, Patrick.
  The last of the old-time cowboys / by Patrick Dearen.
     p.   cm.
  Includes index.
  ISBN 1-55622-613-6
  1. Cowboys—Texas—Bibliography. 2. Cowboys—Texas—
Social life and customs. 3. Ranch life—Texas. 4. Texas—Social
life and customs. I. Title.
  F391.D42   1998
  976.4'06'0922--dc21   98-14583
                                      CIP

ISBN 1-55622-613-6
10 9 8 7 6 5 4 3 2 1
9804

All inquiries for volume purchases of this book should be addressed to Word-
ware Publishing, Inc., at 2320 Los Rios Blvd., Plano, Texas 75074. Telephone
inquiries may be made by calling:
(972) 423-0090

Contents

For my grandmother, Jessie L. Sparkman (1880-1970),
who married a cowboy.

Author's Note

Without the cooperation of scores of old-time cowboys, I could not have written this book. In light of the fact that these men represent the last of their kind, and because their earthy and colorful way of telling a story will soon be lost, I have chosen to let them speak for themselves as much as possible. However, I have edited their comments throughout, occasionally taking minor liberties for the sake of clarity. At times, a quote is a composite of statements made by the individual.

As most of the places named in this book are in Texas, I have included additional identifying information only if a site is outside the state.

Although I have made an effort to verify the spelling of proper names, at times I was unable to do so. A cowboy usually knew a proper name only by the spoken word, not the written page. If any of my spellings are incorrect, the reader is urged to set me straight for later editions of this book.

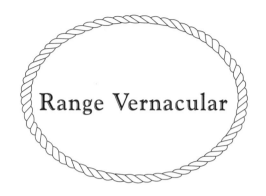

Range Vernacular

Bearcat—(noun), anything a prudent cowboy wouldn't care to tangle with; (adjective), "boarcat," as in "having boarcat hell."

Booger—(noun), anything worthy of a cowhand's fear; (verb), to unnerve.

Break in two—(verb), to begin pitching; said of a horse.

Bronc—(noun), a gelding that is none too gentle.

Catch rope—(noun), a lariat; sometimes spelled "ketch rope."

Chap—(verb), to whip with chaps or leggings.

Corrientes—(noun), wild, cold-blooded Mexican cattle, usually of inferior quality.

Cowpunching—(verb), the act of punching cattle or cowboying.

Cow savvy—(noun), knowledge about cattle.

Cowboy—(verb), to perform the duties of a cowboy.

Daywork—(noun), cowhand work of a temporary nature with wages earned on a daily basis; (verb), to perform such work.

Drag—(noun), the rear of a marching herd.

Drover—(noun), a cowboy who drives cattle.

Dry stock—(noun), any cattle except cows with suckling calves.

Fan—(verb), to slap a horse with a hat (by the rider's own hand).

Flunky—(noun), a cowboy who is assigned menial tasks.

Fork—(verb), to straddle a horse; a "forked rider" is a superb horseman.

Gig—(verb), to spur a horse.

Green-broke—(adjective), ridden only a couple of times before being pastured for the winter; said of a horse.

Greenhorn—(noun), an inexperienced cowboy.

Hackamore—(noun), a halter with a headpiece similar to a bridle, and a band above the horse's mouth in lieu of a bit.

Hooraw—(verb), to tease good-naturedly or celebrate wildly; (noun), the act of teasing or celebrating wildly.

Horse savvy—(noun), knowledge about horses.

Horse jingler—(noun), wrangler; a cowboy who is responsible for the remuda or horse herd.

Horse jingling—(verb), to gather the horse herd.

Job—(verb), to jab or poke.

Kack—(noun), a saddle.

Leggings—(noun), leather coverings for the legs; also known as chaps.

Mill—(verb), to move in a circle; (noun), the act of doing so.

Mixed herd—(noun), a cattle herd which includes bulls, steers, cows, yearlings, and calves, or combinations of such.

Neighbor—(verb), to help out on a nearby ranch, especially during roundup.

Night horse—(noun), a cowboy's gentlest, most dependable horse, reserved solely for night duty, particularly around a cattle herd, and for wrangling the remuda in early morning.

On the peck—(adjective), riled; angered.

Outfit—(noun), a ranch; a group of cowhands engaged in a cattle drive.

Outlaw—(adjective), vicious and untamable; said of a horse or bovine.

Point—(noun), the front of a marching herd; (verb), to perform the duties of a cowboy riding point.

Remuda—(noun), a saddle horse herd.

Rustle—(verb), to gather; said of the remuda.

Salty—(adjective), unyielding and displaying plenty of fight.

Screw down—(verb), to sit as deep as possible in the saddle and dig spurs into the cinch.

Snaky—(adjective), treacherous; said of a horse.

Spook—(verb), to unnerve.

Stray man—(noun), a cowboy who represents his home ranch's brand at another outfit's roundup; also known as a "rep."

Sunfish—(verb), to twist side-to-side while pitching; said of a horse.

Swallow his head—(verb), to lower the head as a prelude to pitching; said of a horse.

Tally book—(noun), a small book for keeping careful record of cattle.

Tenderfoot—(noun), a person new to the cowboy life; (verb), to act as a tenderfoot.

Top hand—(noun), a cowhand respected for his experience and ability.

Trail-broke—(adjective), broken in to life on the trail; said of a cattle herd.

Trap—(noun), a fenced area much larger than a typical corral.

Water-gapping—(verb), to maintain and repair the sections of a fence that cross a drainage.

Windy—(adjective), prone to spinning tall tales or talking excessively, especially in a boastful, know-it-all manner.

Wormy—(adjective), plagued by screwworms; (noun), a bovine suffering from such a condition.

Saddling Up

At a lonely line camp deep in chiseled Palo Duro Canyon, where the "Big Red" snakes through the Texas Panhandle, ninety-one-year-old Tom Blasingame dug his boot into the stirrup one last time.

By the world's reckoning, it was December 27, 1989, and overhead, hidden beyond the blue of the sky, satellites raced by in silent orbit. Somewhere over the red-tinged buttes on the horizon, pickups bounced along ranch roads and cattle trucks roared down superhighways. Fencing crews strung barbed wire, and mechanics tuned up helicopters and motorcycles, readying them for spring roundups. The old ways were mere ghosts now, but in this rugged backcountry of the JA Ranch co-founded by Charles Goodnight in 1877, time stood still for likely America's oldest working cowboy. It could have been 1916, when an eighteen-year-old Blasingame rode up on an iron-gray horse and signed on with the JA's to help seventeen other cowhands work 25,000 mother cows.

Alone now, with nothing but crow's-feet and sagging shoulders to betray the passage of years, Blasingame turned his horse away from his primitive line shack near Campbell Creek and rode again into a sprawling country fit for a cowboy. He broke trail through the brush unaware of the burden he shouldered, for he was the lone remnant of the last-of-a-breed men who had cowboyed before mechanization. They had taken up life in the saddle in the first third of the twentieth century, and every time a hand like Blasingame had forked a wild bronc or roped an ornery steer, he had carried on the traditions of Goodnight and other cowhands from out of the old rock.

Tom Blasingame at his JA Ranch line camp in 1989.

Like those who already had passed on, to stove-up lives of dependence or to pastures beyond the sky, Blasingame had seen it all—the trail drives and pummeling storms, the lightning-eared horses and mill of spooked cattle, the thundering stampedes and hellbent-for-leather chases, the brutal horse wrecks and deadly draggings. His generation had been the last to live a coyote's life out of a line camp or chuck wagon, where a cowhand might face humor and hoo-rawing one moment and the strike of a rattler or devil-horned cow the next. By World War II, technology and the pickup had changed all of that, but on this winter day, Blasingame hugged a saddle and gripped reins in unconscious homage to his dying breed.

Prowling the breaks near Bull Run Creek, a tributary of the Big Red, he evidently realized he was in trouble. Dismounting, he stretched out on his back in the Palo Duro grass at the hooves of his horse. With feet firm in his boots, he folded his arms across his chest, closed his eyes to the fading sun of the Old West, and died the way a cowboy should.

But he and his kind had a legacy as strong as stout saddle leather—to live on as genuine legends who had ridden through a golden moment in American history.

In the 1980s, I went looking for the last of these aging icons who had emerged from the wellspring of cowboy-ing—Texas and eastern New Mexico. Time was not on my side. By then, any man old enough to have cowboyed before mechanization would have been pushing at least eighty, even if he had straddled his first green-broke horse as a kid. More likely, he would have been closer to ninety or a hundred. Nevertheless, during the next few years I rode a fascinating trail that took me to the craggy faces of dozens of onetime cowhands whose squinting eyes and quavering voices seemed young again as they spoke of the old days.

Tom Blasingame I talked with under a leafy elm alive with the buzz of cicadas, there at his line camp in the heart of Palo Duro Canyon. Others I visited in their modest homes, on sunlit porches, in grassy yards, or in small-town cafes. I captured the story of one remarkable cowhand while he was wheelchair-bound in a nursing home. I corralled another throwback in the last few days of an extraordinary life that spanned ninety-five years and two centuries. In my frantic race against the clock, I drove thousands of miles, and as the dark midnight of the Old West fell, I finished bridging the gulf between today and yesteryear with a symbol of technology—the telephone.

By the time my ride was over, I had tracked down and roped the stories of seventy-six old-time cowhands, fifty-four of them in face-to-face roundups. Of that seventy-six, three were born before 1895, twelve in the period 1896-1900 (inclusive), twenty in 1901-1905, thirty-one in 1906-1910, and ten in 1911-1915. The two oldest took up cowboying as very young hands at the close of the nineteenth century, and the rest mounted up no later than 1931.

The author and 1920s cowhand Paul Patterson at Castle Gap in 1994. (courtesy, Ed Todd)

Their stories consumed scores of hours of audio tape, and in selectively transcribing, I found unfolding before my eyes a thousand pages of priceless material otherwise destined to disappear like the need for night horses or lead steers. I could almost taste the horse sweat with every word, for these were not cowboys of the celluloid, urban, or Dallas variety; these were genuine, honest-to-goodness cowhands who stood tall in the saddle as the prototypes of an American myth.

Their names—Buck, Gid, Bud, Green, Si, Shorty, Slim, Fish—often rang with color, and their spellbinding stories spoke of a simpler era when a man's word was his bond and a cowhand rode hard and lived harder. A half-century after most had hung up their spurs, each still clung to the memories like a seasoned hand to a sunfishing bronc on a frosty morning. To be sure, the beckoning sunset was inescapable for even the saltiest cowpuncher, but one and all have now found a new dawn in these pages.

In a bunkhouse, at a line camp, around a chuck wagon —there, to the creak of a sagging floor, the low of a night herd, the crackle of a mesquite fire, they first spun these long-dormant tales. An impressionable tenderfoot probably would have taken every last detail and each snippet of lore as gospel truth. A hand a little wiser to the ways of the range probably would have kept in mind the observation of cowpuncher Frank Yeary: "They's been more wild and mean horses rode sitting on that bedroll around the campfire than any other place in the world." Still, greenhorn and top hand alike would have listened equally wide-eyed, for these stories bear the unmistakable brand of an Old West that is now but a dusty grave on a long-lost trail.

Roping the Wind

They worked from *you can till you can't*, to the howl of stinging sandstorms or the drum of hard white rocks falling from the sky. They sweated under a firebrand sun or shivered to the chill of a blizzard, coughed to the rasp of alkali crawling down their throats, or winced to the driving rain beating out a somber cadence against hat brims. And sometimes, when the dark sky was rent by lightning, they shuddered to the eerie spikes of fire that torched the cattle's horns or the ears of the very horses on which they rode.

And throughout their long, hard ride, the last old-time cowboys had no forewarning of meteorologic changes except that which their own folklore told them was true.

Foremost, they looked to the very animals that defined their lives—horses and cattle, whose instincts, while beyond understanding, proved virtually unerring.

"Animals are smarter than human beings," observed Orval Sparks, who began cowboying about 1925 in Concho County. "A horse can tell you more about what the weather's going to be than the weatherman."

Bill Shields, who forked many a bronc from the time he first hired out in 1917, saw for himself the horse's remarkable sensitivity to a threatening sky: "If a cloud's bad, an ol' horse will go to shaking his head, watching that cloud. They can really tell you—if it ain't a bad cloud, they won't notice it."

With its inbred barometer, a horse could tell a cowboy plenty even in face of a cloudless horizon.

"They'll throw their nose up and look to the north and snort," noted Sparks. "That mean's it's a-comin' a norther. And if it's going to rain, well, they start running in circles."

Of all the meteorologic signs in western folklore, cowhands gave the most credence to this tendency of horses to run prior to impending weather changes. Shorty Northcutt, who learned his horse savvy as a mere kid-of-a-hand in the mid-1920s, further detailed their predictive actions. "A lot of times," he said, "horses just break a-loose and run—run in a circle, pitch and play."

Added cowhand Charlie Drennan, "A horse will go to kicking up his heels."

Such playful manner, including pawing, on the part of the remuda was interpreted variously by cowboys. While some ranch hands merely prepared for a general change in the weather, discerning cowboys considered the time of year and looked for specific changes. If the rainy season (such as it was in this arid region) was at hand, they joined Sparks in readying their slickers for a light sprinkle or hard downpour. In thunderstorm season, they feared the onslaught of fierce winds, pounding hail, and deadly lightning. And from fall through early spring, they tied their cowhide coats on the backs of their saddles and prepared to shiver.

Forty-seven-year-old Olan George, cowboying near Fort Stockton on a warm November day in 1955, was the principal in a dramatic instance of reading a coming blizzard in the actions of horses. Recalled George:

Olan George in 1989.

You just didn't see a late-fall day any prettier. We were in our shirt-sleeves, and we had just worked a couple of hundred head of cattle. We came in just before sundown and the horses were all tired and we were tired. We unsaddled our horses and turned them in the pen. All of a sudden—it looked like on a signal—those horses all just turned a handspring and went to pitching and running and playing and biting at one another. You wouldn't've thought they'd done a hard day's work.

A young Texas A&M University graduate by the name of Norman turned to George, who had been well schooled in the ways of saddle stock from boyhood. "Mr. George," asked Norman, "what's stung those horses?"

I said, "Norman, there ain't nothing stung 'em—they're just predicting the weather, that's all." And he said, "Well, if they're so smart, what's the weather going to do?" I said, "Norman, in the morning, when you wake up, there'll be about four inches of snow right here on the ground where we're standing."

Well, he just guffawed me. He laughed [as if to say], "I wish you'd listen to that old man—not a cloud in the sky, not even a warning of anything. Him and them horses are crazy."

At four o'clock the next morning, a knock on the door roused George from bed. Answering the summons, he found the A&M graduate standing with his back to a raging blizzard that already had deposited three inches of snow. "Mr. George," said the befuddled young man, "get up and put your clothes on—I want to buy your breakfast. You've got something that I want to *know*."

Sometimes a cowhand could foresee an onrushing cold front by studying a horse's physical appearance. "Their tails and mane would be a-stickin' out," related   Jack

Cauble, who first began dayworking in eastern New Mexico about 1923. "On the tail, especially, you'd notice it." Leonard Hernandez, who was breaking horses as early as 1920, described this portending tail as "fluffy, like somebody'd brushed it."

Presenting much the look of a wind-blown animal, an anticipating horse even offered clues to the wintry blast's time of arrival. "If you went out kind of late in the evening," noted longtime cowhand Ted Powers, "and the ol' horse's tail was all flared up, a norther would be there by morning."

In preparation for the strike of a cold front, horses were known to lie down and rest at a time they normally grazed. If a severe winter storm were on the way, they signaled it to veteran cowhands by drifting south and seeking a windbreak or, in the absence of brush, by bunching. At times, however, horses' instincts to gain safe ground indicated not a cold snap, but a flash flood.

"I used to work on this ranch out at Monument Switch [southwest of Mertzon], and I'd rustle horses every morning," recalled Paul Patterson. "That big ol' draw there would get fifteen feet deep [with runoff]. Two or three days before a rain, the horses would run up on top of a hill, and it'd come a heck of a rain. [The other hands] said, 'Well, the reason they did that was because the flies got so bad.' I said, 'All right, how do the *flies* know it's going to rain?' I like to believe that it's the horses—I don't want to believe it's the flies."

Equally sensitive to the sovereign ways of nature were cattle, which foretold weather changes in ways both similar to horses and unique. Even more so than the remuda, a herd seemed to know just when to prepare for a coming bad spell.

"When you see a bunch of cattle laying down [from morning through mid-day], well, you better look out—it's gonna come something," noted Hudson "Bud" Mayes, who first hired out as a cowboy in 1909.

This unusual rest period precipitated a weather swing that often was dramatic, with seasonal conditions giving way to a storm or heavy rain or the teeth of a brutal norther. Taking note of the cattle's actions, an experienced cowhand could ready himself for whatever lay in store.

"In the wintertime, if there's not a cow standing up, you can figure on something coming up that night," noted Ted Laughlin, a dollar-a-day cowboy in eastern New Mexico as early as 1926.

"They'll all be laying down and chewing their cud and resting all they can," added Max Reed of the old Scharbauer outfit on the Texas South Plains.

More specifically, a cowboy could take it as an omen if a herd came in for water early on a winter morning and bedded down by 10 A.M. or 11 A.M. If the brewing storm was still eighteen to twenty-four hours away, the cattle might continue their respite until evening. But when they rose, it was to cast a knowing look to the clueless horizon and prepare to retreat. Recalled Olan George:

"If you can see that ol' cow look toward the north and stretch her body, get just as high off the ground with that body as she can, even on tiptoes, and smell, and then directly wring that tail and go to running—you look out.

Before ten hours are gone, there's going to be some kind of weather change."

Before bolting, cattle often gave further warning of the approach of a storm or norther.

"They'd just go to acting peculiar," said Wood Whatley, who worked his share of cattle in Texas and Colorado. "They'd just sort of mill around and throw their heads up and sort of snort."

"Those cattle," added early 1930s hand Buck Murrah, "will go to bawling and they'll go to milling. That means they're getting restless; they're going to run."

Lee Brice on the Jake McClure Ranch near Lovington, New Mexico, in the 1930s. (courtesy, Lee Brice)

When they ran, it was not in stampede, but in unusual frolic, bucking and kicking up heels much like horses. If a severe winter storm threatened, a herd's actions grew more calculating.

"Cows would begin to move to different places and they'd bawl a lot," related Lee Brice, who took up cowboying near Lovington, New Mexico, in 1929. "They wouldn't bunch up."

Most important to cattle at such a time was the need to flee the surging norther. "They'll be wanting to go south and get wherever the protection is," said Vance Davis, a hand by age twelve in 1918.

Sometimes the instinct to escape a fierce blizzard sent cattle afar. During the era of large pastures (sometimes 100 sections) in the early twentieth century, this inevitably forced cattle to bunch up against south-lying fences and perhaps die. But back in the open-range days of 1884 to 1885, tens of thousands of anticipating cattle drifted south-southwest from the Panhandle and, even as the icy blast overtook them, pushed on 300 to 400 miles to the lower Pecos River. It was the largest mass drift in the annals of the West.

Less dramatic but equally fascinating was a bovine's ability to forecast a downpour by displaying odd physical mannerisms. Related cowhand Gaston Boykin: "I heard a fellow talking about when to tell if it was going to rain—a cow would go to walking like she was walking in mud." In perhaps a similar observation, 1920s hand Tom Parisher pointed out the tendency of a cow to "stick out her hind foot and shake it" prior to a rain.

In addition to short-term forecasts, cattle and horses offered long-term indicators. Most telling was the degree of hair growth triggered by some inner mechanism.

"In some years the cattle would have a thick growth of hair, and so would the horses," remembered Marvin Beauchamp, who began cowboying near Odessa in 1930. "That would supposedly mean a bad winter."

A cowhand could also read much into how early the livestock began putting on their winter coat. Said South Texas cowhand Otis Coggins:

"If it's going to be a bad winter, they'd put a coat of hair on earlier, say, along in November. It was according to what country you was in. Out in this [Trans-Pecos] country, they're liable to start putting their hair on [for a bad winter] the last part of September, first of November. Down there in South Texas, it's liable to be close to December, first of January, before they'd have a real heavy coat."

Bulls, while sharing this trait, gave observant cowboys even more reason to seal the cracks in the line shacks. "If it's going to be a hard winter," noted Paul Patterson, "old bulls leave cows alone earlier [in the breeding season]. I guess they build up their strength."

By the early twentieth century, cowboys such as Louis Baker sometimes found themselves involved with sheep outfits, whose herders passed along additional weather lore.

"One day [near Mertzon in 1924], the sheep was grazing going up the hill up high, and we was wanting them to stay back down at the bottom," recalled Baker, who was working with an old Mexican herder at the time. "'No,' he says, 'pretty soon *mucho* rain.' Well, it was just pretty all over then. But in about three hours, it come a flood down there. Man, it sure did rain."

The sheepherder also taught Baker to anticipate dramatic shifts in wind direction. "He told me, 'When that wind's out of the north, sheep will travel north [as they graze]. If that wind's going to change and come from the

19

south, three or four hours before then, they'll turn back and start going to the south.'"

Other domestic animals, as well, proved excellent indicators. In advance of a bad spell, noted some hands, not only did the hogs at headquarters build nests, but goats invariably joined cattle and horses in resting or seeking protection.

To a cowboy immersed in range only a few years removed from wilderness, the native wildlife also loomed as a weather barometer. Chief among the signs was the mournful howl of a coyote.

"When coyotes is a-howlin' in daytime," related cowhand L. Kinser, "it's gonna be bad weather."

Other cowhands found significance in a howl that came at a different time. If coyotes were vocal during the night, Chon Villalba (a cowboy by 1915) looked for a cold snap by daybreak, while Fred McClellan (a hand by 1925) braced for a change if the canines delayed "raising hell" till morning.

Another denizen whose actions revealed much in certain regions was the antelope. When Marvin Hooper began dayworking on the open range of eastern New Mexico in the early 1910s, he quickly learned to dread a sudden passage of the animals. "You let it get real bad on up north and those antelope will go to coming by there going south," he noted. "Whenever they go to drifting by, you can bet your dollar there's something coming behind."

Cowboys also considered the ways of birds. They knew the nocturnal hoot of an owl and the fall migration of southbound geese and cranes as indications of impending cold, while precipitation lurked if a rain crow called or if a vulture exhibited a certain odd mannerism. Observed Tom Parisher: "If a buzzard's sitting on a fence post a-scratchin' hisself, it's gonna rain."

Ground species, often shunned and even feared by cowboys, nevertheless gained respect for their own weather insights. A drenching rain, in particular, always seemed to follow the appearance of abundant terrapins, toad frogs, and, especially, rattlesnakes on the move. Sometimes, the actions of even a single rattler proved valuable.

"If he's going out of a creek, it's gonna rain," said Parisher. "If he's going up a hill, if he's getting away from a low place, that's a sign of rain. Sometimes it'll be two or three days, but he knows that."

Anytime, in fact, that ground species took to high ground or to trees, cowhands such as Lonnie Griffith considered it a "guaranteed sign."

"When you see frogs, tarantulas, snakes, lizards, and horned frogs going up a tree, in about three days you'll have a rain," he noted.

Cowboying on his stepfather's ranch in Borden County in the 1910s, Griffith witnessed just such an omen of a gully-washer. He recalled:

> One day we was riding down through some pretty good-sized trees. Dad was right ahead of me 'cause the trail was kind of narrow. I happened to look up ahead of him and I saw an ol' rattlesnake hanging down about as long as my arm. He had his head hanging down and he had his ol' head drawed back, and Dad was riding right into him and he

wasn't looking up; he was watching the trail. I yelled at him and he wheeled his horse [to] one side and went under that snake. And that snake, I thought, struck, but he didn't hit him 'cause he was a good three feet above Dad's head on a horse.

Complementing the signs exhibited by creatures were atmospheric indicators. It was common, in fact, for cowboys to look to current conditions in order to predict future patterns.

Thunder seemed a prime omen. "If you hear it thunder before seven in the day," noted P. O. "Slim" Vines, a hand by 1924, "it'll rain before eleven." Furthermore, every cowboy seemed to know the old adage, "Thunder in February, frost in April (or May)."

The wind could also be a portent. "We always said when these little northers kept coming, way up in the spring—we called them *dry northers*—it was going to be a dry year," remembered Joe Lambert, who was born on a ranch near Rotan in 1899 and grew up cowboying.

The wind did not limit its foreshadowing to spring. Recalled Parisher: "If it was in the wintertime or fall, you could tell [by the] way the wind was from whether it was gonna be cold or not. If it was from the north or east, it was gonna rain or be cold. If it was from the south, it would generally be foggy."

To cowhands such as Walter Hoelscher, fog itself was a noteworthy sign, presaging a heavy rain in ninety days. But when the vapor broke, other cowboys lifted their gazes to the sky and divined even more. While some found truth in the old proverb, "Red sky at night, sailors delight; red sky at morning, sailors take warning," others gleaned very specific information from the sun and clouds. Offered Vines: "If the sun sets behind a cloud on Sunday night, it'll rain before Wednesday night."

J. E. "Shorty" Northcutt in 1989.

Shorty Northcutt learned to wait until sunrise for a prime sign to develop:

> We was working down on the south side [of the Spade Ranch near Colorado City] and I remember that morning, early, why, the sun come up and then went back to bed [went behind a cloud bank]. One of these old men said, "You better look out, she's gonna come a gully-washer today, 'cause when that

sun comes up clear and then goes back to bed, look out."

And that morning, everybody was off killing rattlesnakes—about as good a sign as you can get. And about noon, sure enough, we got a gully-washer.

Clouds alone were enough to inform keen observers of all they needed to know. Fleecy clouds promised rain in three days, and white clouds with "mare tails" meant a change of unspecified nature. Likewise, broken clouds with an indigo sky behind were cause for concern.

Then, of course, every cowhand worth his salt knew the sign of an imminent "blue norther"—a northern horizon painted a deep violet-blue. Sometimes, however, a cowboy had to be sure of what he saw, as Slim Vines learned in 1931 when, seeking horses, he rode from the plains of Midland to the rugged country of southeastern New Mexico.

"I was going across those sand hills up there," he recalled, "and I could see a heck of a cloud back in the northwest. In those days, if we ever got a big rain out of the northwest, it was a soaker. So I got up there [to stay overnight at a ranch en route] and there was an old man there. I told him, 'I've run into a shower or two since I left home. I been worrying about this cloud back in the northwest.' He said, 'Well, I never noticed it. I didn't know there was a cloud coming up.' I said, 'Yeah, it looked pretty rainy—I hope I don't get in a cloud tomorrow and get wet.'"

The next morning, Vines rose to study the northwest horizon again. "Well," he complained, "there's that cloud still back in there."

"I don't see any cloud," said his host.

"Can't you see low down in there how blue it is? That looks like a heck of a thunderstorm to me."

His host's jaw dropped. "Why that's not a cloud!" he exclaimed, turning to the flatland cowboy. "That's the Guadalupe Mountains!"

Looming cloud banks, real or otherwise, were always worrisome. When Bill Shields was a young hand on his first cowboying job near Vernon in 1917, he learned a valuable lesson from an aging cowhand whose craggy face told of a hard ride through the 1800s. "Son," said the old-timer, "you see that bank coming up? If that backs off tonight, we're okay, but when it comes on over you, you better look out—it'll be a bearcat."

Even a clear sky could seize a knowledgeable cowboy's attention. Not only was a cloudless day considered a "weather breeder" at particular times of year, but folklore held that certain clear nights in early winter indicated dry months to come.

"Starting Christmas, they watched those nights," noted Walter Hoelscher. "Every night would [represent] a different month, from January on. If Christmas night was clear, then it wouldn't rain in January. But if the second night was cloudy, then it should rain in February. And so on."

Many cowboys also swore by signs in the moon. Like the sun, a moon rising red was reason to take precautions—perhaps against an oncoming arctic storm. Another omen of cold was when "a big moon" began rising increasingly to the north of east, noted L. E. Davis. Evidently, this was in late September or early October at harvest moon, when the early evening full (or nearly so) moon, viewed at the same hour on several successive nights, appeared to have moved northward along the eastern horizon. More weather signs lay in the moon's phases, which seemed to foreshadow periods of wet and dryness. Some cowhands believed it wouldn't rain during "the dark of the moon" or on a bright, moonlit night, especially one with a full moon. Others pointed to the first quarter as favorable for a cloudburst, depending on the angle of the sinking crescent to the western horizon. Explained Steve Armentrout:

"If it's setting on its back, it's a-holdin' the water; it's not going to rain. If it's over there on the point, it's pouring out the water; it's going to rain."

The moon and stars in combination yielded a much more specific forecast.

"I stayed out at a sheep camp with an old Mexican one time a long time ago," recalled Bud Mayes. "He could tell what it was going to do the next two or three days—he'd watch the stars and the moon. When there was a big circle [halo] around the moon, if there was a star or two in it, that was how many days it'd be before it rained."

Stars figured prominently in other weather lore as well. A halo around a lone star in winter promised snow, while rain was imminent if the Big Dipper were on end or upside-down and "pouring out water." Similarly, noted cowhand Leonard Hernandez, wet or dry conditions were indicated at certain times of year by the position of a plow-shaped group of stars (otherwise unidentified by Hernandez) in the early night sky.

Sometimes a discerning cowboy predicted the weather in a more down-to-earth way—by slitting an Irish potato, putting it in water, and studying its reaction over a period of time. Too, there was the sure-bet indicator known to every stove-up old cowboy.

"Those crippled-up old cowpunchers—some of them seventy, eighty years—they had lots of broken bones," recalled Thomas Henderson, who grew up on ranches in the Big Bend in the 1910s. "Lots of times they'd tell you [by the feeling in their joints] when it was going to come up a cold spell or rain."

Despite the cowboy's general reliance on weather signs, there were some cowpunchers who believed that predicting the weather was like trying to rope the wind.

"They said, 'The dry ones worked in dry weather and the wet ones worked in wet weather, and the rest of them you couldn't depend on,'" related Slim Vines.

Furthermore, old-fashioned "horse sense" sometimes prevailed over the farfetched.

"My daddy didn't think it'd rain when the moon was shining so bright," said onetime Pecos River hand Walter Boren. Indeed, one long-ago night found the younger Boren studying a big West Texas moon and a starry sky, which, true to prediction, held not a hint of rain. Nevertheless, his brother-in-law pointed out a cogent fact: "It's dry here and just raining like hell down in Galveston [on the Texas coast]. They got the same moon down there we have here, don't they?"

Moreover, claimed some cowboys, signs that a fellow once could have bet his last dollar on would have put him in the poor house later on.

"When a cow would start kicking, they'd say, 'Well, we're gonna get some rain,'" remembered Leonard Hernandez. "And now she can kick her foot off, it *still* don't rain. But long time ago it sure did work."

Borden County cowboy Lonnie Griffith attributed the decline in accuracy of such signs to man's meddling with the environment.

"We used to guarantee it [would rain] if we saw a cloud coming from the northwest," he recalled. "It'd come up in the evening and disappear and then next day it'd come up and disappear, and then the third day you saw it coming, you'd better duck. We could might near bet on them things, and I have, a-many a times. But since they shot the atomic bomb over at White Sands [Missile Range in New Mexico in 1945], why, we don't get that no more."

About the only weather indicator that truly was certain in any era was what cowboys knew as the old Indian sign for rain: "When it's cloudy all around and pouring down the middle."

Douglas Poage, who hired on with the OH Triangle Ranch near Mertzon in 1922, related a story about perhaps this same apocryphal Indian. Cowboying on a spread in more modern times, the Indian displayed an extraordinary ability to predict the weather. Every morning his fellow hands would ask him for the day's forecast, and invariably he would give an answer that proved correct. Everyone was amazed at the way he had inherited such insight into nature from his wild forebears; here was a throwback who was as much a part of nature as the very wind and clouds.

Then came a morning when the cowhands asked for a forecast, only to see the Indian shrug. "How would I know?" he replied. "My radio was broke."

Bracing themselves for the bite of a brutal storm, cowboys needed not only the memory of a good laugh, but all the courage they could muster.

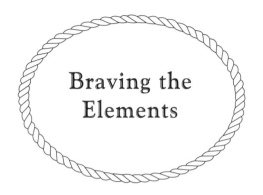

Braving the Elements

Despite anticipating a meteorologic change, cowboys seldom were able to plan around it, not in a job that demanded such close ties with livestock and nature. In fact, about the only task in which the weather could be prohibitive was branding, which required conditions suitable for a fire.

"Our outfit, they just drawed a circle around a number on the calendar and that's the day they was gonna work and the weather didn't make any difference," recalled Max Reed, who signed on with the Scharbauer Cattle Company near Midland about 1927.

The most common form of inclement weather that cowboys faced was rain, which, despite the region's aridity, could deal a hand a lot of misery. Still, if he were driving or holding a herd, he had no choice but to slip on a worn slicker and tough it out.

"If you get caught in one of them storms," said longtime hand Bill Townsend, "you stay with them cattle, regardless."

Seth Young proved his mettle early, as a mere ten-year-old on a cattle drive in 1912 or 1913. Helping his father and three other drovers push 200 to 250 head from Rocksprings southwest to Del Rio, he stayed in the saddle through a long, wet ordeal.

"It rained for three days straight, but we had nothing to do but take it and go on," he remembered. "I was riding a little gray, bald-faced horse and I hated for my saddle to get wet. I had a man's slicker on, and I spread it over my saddle so that the horn came up between the buttons. We was driving cattle and I slid off and I forgot to unbutton that button or lift it off, and I just hung to it. This ol' horse just whirled around and around till that button hole tore off that slicker and down I went."

The nights were as soggy and miserable as the days. "I slept under the wagon every night with my daddy," recalled Young, "but we slept about half wet—the rain would blow in on you."

Although a wagon camp with its bedrolls and tarps offered a rain-chilled drover his only hope for a comfortable night, sleeping in a downpour was always trying.

"Out at a chuck wagon, if it come up a rain or storm at night, the boss would make everybody get up and roll their beds up," remembered L. B. "Bill" Eddins, who first hired out about 1914 in the Pecos River country. "Those [bedroll] tarps, they'll get soaked up and then they'll turn water, but your bed's already wet when it does that. There's nothing in the world any heavier than a ol' rolled-up wet bed. It'll bring a wagon down by the time you get ten or fifteen beds wet. Some of these ol' kids wouldn't want to, but he'd make them get up, roll their bed up, and pile them up on there. We'd put slickers on till it quit raining and then go back to bed."

Sometimes a drenched rider wished mighty hard for just such an inconvenience, as drovers Olan George and Ead Powell learned upon riding out of a chuck wagon camp near Fort Stockton in the 1920s. Delivering a small herd of cattle to a ranch in nearby Leon Valley, the two men started back, only to be overtaken by dark and a storm.

"It was raining right straight down," remembered George. "It seemed like the longer we stayed out, the harder it rained. By the time we got back to the [camp's] location, it was about 11 o'clock and we couldn't find the chuck wagon. It was so dark that you couldn't see your hand, and the ol' cook had gone to bed and failed to leave a light. Usually [a cook] would put a cover over the chuck box and put a lantern under it so we could see it.

"We hunted a good two hours before we ever found that chuck wagon. And Ead, a slow-talking ol' cowboy, he walked over and jerked that cook out of bed and he worked him over good—'Don't you *ever*, not one time the rest of your life if a man's out working at night, fail to put a lantern on that box!' I never did get warm all night."

Even if every precaution was taken, cowboys faced the danger of hypothermia or serious illness every time they worked for extended periods in the rain. Just such a trial greeted L. Kinser and other SMS hands when they headed out with the roundup wagon from near Paducah one autumn Sunday in the 1920s. For the next six days it rained around the clock, keeping everything so soaked that "you couldn't even get your boots on," recalled Kinser. Not until they pulled into ranch headquarters the following Saturday did the downpour relent. By then, two hands had come down seriously ill, with one fated to die of pneumonia.

Sometimes even unseen rain could cause problems. One sunny day in the 1910s, Lonnie Griffith took his mount across the Colorado River in Borden County in search of stray horses on the bordering OB Ranch. Rounding up the animals, he drove them back to the river, which normally was so tame that it had no surface flow between water holes. This day, however, it was a different story.

"The durned thing was almost a half-mile wide and we hadn't even saw a cloud or heard any thunder or seen any lightning or anything," said Griffith. "So I was trapped over there. I went over to the OB Ranch and stayed over there four days before I could get across."

Even more trying than wet spells were arctic fronts, which could threaten an exposed cowhand in several ways. "One night we was out with a bunch of cattle, holding them, and it come up a norther," remembered Bill Eddins. "And we was just as cold as the dickens—it was blowing hard, spitting rain, dust flying."

This combination of wind, moisture, and frigid temperatures could actually numb a cowboy astride a horse. Recalled Brewster County cowhand Clarence Arrott: "In the wintertime it'd get so cold you couldn't sit on your horse, or you'd freeze on him and you couldn't get off. You'd have to twist around and slide off."

On January 17, 1930, Panhandle cowboy Frank Yeary knew just such a feeling. "It was the coldest day that I was ever out in my life," he recalled. "I come nearer to freezing to death that day than I ever did or ever will. Me and Henry Murrell left the [Lewis and Letts] ranch that morning at five o'clock and it was snowing and a-blowin'. And then we got in about three that evening and they had to come out and take me off my horse. I couldn't get off—I was froze to my saddle. And old Doctor Garner at Turkey told me that my ears would come off just like a froze-eared calf. They was just as black as a hat. But they didn't. Still got 'em—proud of 'em."

Clarence Arrott in 1917.

One hundred fifty miles southwest near Andrews, evidently the same storm caught seventeen-year-old Shorty Northcutt unawares. Trailing three bulls ten or twelve miles across the exposed plains en route to Sand Ranch, he was engulfed by a norther.

"Man, it just kept a-gettin' colder and colder," he remembered. "When I got about halfway to the ranch down there, why, I come to a trap [fenced area]. And I just put these bulls in that trap and then I just loped [my horse] on to the ranch. And boy, it just froze my feet something terrible."

Nevertheless, Northcutt could not content himself with recovering. The next day, he dragged himself back out in the cold and saddled his horse. "I went over to get my bulls and bring them in and they was all three dead, just laying there with their heads around to the side. They just went inside [the trap] and just laid down, and that's as far as they got."

Sometimes, though, a cowboy could find a certain beauty in a winter storm. Rounding up forty-three outlaw mares in a falling snow on the Davidson Ranch near Ozona in December 1925, Green Mankin and Charlie Davidson witnessed a unique meteorologic effect as they came upon a pair of paint stallions that considered the men a threat.

"Them ol' horses [stallions] would stand on their feet and rear up and paw in the air," recalled Mankin. "It was kind of raining, just like rainbows in the air. You could see rainbows on the horses and on the ground and just right up against everything. Them ol' horses run out on the side of that hill, rearing up there and rainbows everywhere, and it was the prettiest sight."

Nevertheless, the fury of a winter storm could be deadly, even for a seasoned hand. When sixty-nine-year-old Jack Pate rode out with a pack outfit to feed hungry cattle in a remote canyon in Mora County, New Mexico, in 1973, he carried the experience of more than a half-century in the saddle. Still, even as the wintry slopes of the Sangre de Cristo Mountains rose up around him, nothing could have prepared him for the onslaught he was about to face.

"I knew we had a storm a-comin', but it was supposed to hit that night and it come in early," he remembered. "In three minutes you couldn't see your hand in front of you, that snow was blowing so hard."

Hopelessly disoriented, Pate could do only one thing—give his horse its head and trust its instincts. "I was riding a smart horse that time, an ol' horse called Brownie. And he was the horse that took me home."

Even so, Pate paid a heavy price in frostbite. "The next morning," he recalled, "I had to get hot towels to get my eyes open. All the skin come off my face. If it hadn't been for that ol' horse, I wouldn't've got home."

One of the most dreaded forms of severe weather was a hailstorm, which could swoop down with vicious force before a cowboy had a chance to seek shelter or even dismount. Often, he had time only to pull his hat down tight, hump across the saddle horn, and grit his teeth to the hard rocks falling furiously from the sky. Even as he endured the battering, he had to retain the presence of mind to control his crazed horse, which knew only to turn its rump to the storm.

"You had to 'stay with him,'" said Bill Townsend, using a cowhand term for coping with an ornery horse. "He'd really cut up."

Back in 1929 Townsend was riding pasture in Arthur Hoover's Live Oak Ranch in Crockett County when he faced just such a challenge.

"We'd just get out and prowl and hunt for wormies [cattle with screwworms], and it just come up one of them little ol' quick clouds about three o'clock in the evening," Townsend recalled. "It was right on top of you before you knew it and you didn't have time to get nowhere. It lasted about three, four minutes. My horse didn't like it. There was lots of little bitty hail and every now and then one of them ol' big ones, as big as golf balls, and that's what skinned you up. I had blue spots all over my arm. I guess my back was blue too."

At best, a cowboy in the grip of such a storm could count on reshaping his battered hat. At worst, his skull might fracture under an assault of stones as big as his fist, as seventeen-year-old Lonnie Griffith and two other hands feared as they approached a Borden County ranch with 1,500 sheep about 1921.

Lonnie Griffith in 1983.

"There was an old man with me and Dad, and we was walking, leading our horses," related Griffith. "We'd been riding them, but now we was just driving these sheep and walking along. When this hail first hit, why, them horses jerked loose and run off with their saddles. Usually, we'd take the saddle off the horse, leave the blanket on the horse for a little protection, and we'd hold the saddle up over our backs and our heads.

"Well, they got away and I never saw such a hail in my life, big ol' stones about golf ball-sized. There wasn't even a tree or a bush or nothing there, so Dad, he just kind of wrapped me up under him, tucked my head in his shoulders."

All three drovers realized their peril, but, cowboy-like, they suppressed their fear as the hail pounded down.

"Don't your mother wish she knew how good we was getting along?" Griffith's stepfather asked him wryly as they huddled on the ground.

Meanwhile, the older cowhand, squatting nearby, winced and doubled over as a huge hailstone caught him flush. "God, Old Man," he said, "You better not do that again—You'll get this fellow."

Fortunately, the storm passed within minutes, leaving the drovers bruised and afoot but alive.

In a barren country, the best a cowboy could hope for under the threat of hail was time enough to unsaddle his horse and tie his catch-rope to the bridle reins. Hanging on desperately to the spooked animal, he might crouch under the stout saddle leather and gain a measure of protection as the stones hopped about him like a swarm of strange, white insects. Even if there were a few scrub limbs above him, he seldom came out unscathed, especially if, in the storm's aftermath, his saddle looked as if a blacksmith had taken a ball peen hammer to it.

Lewis Doran, facing a menacing cloud on a Concho County ranch about 1929, luckily had a knowledgeable cowhand riding at his side. He related:

Me and my daddy was out in the pasture coming home, and we saw this cloud coming up pretty fast. He told me, "Now, I think it's hail in that cloud—it's too red. Let's get up there at that thicket, pull our saddles off, and tie our roping rope to the reins so the horses won't run off. Back up in that thicket there and put the blanket over your head and then put the saddle over your head. And you can take that hail."

So we did, and about the time we got everything fixed in that thicket, well, here it come. Man, it was falling fast and hard. It mashed one of my fingers—I had my hand up through a place in my saddle—but that was the only bruise I got. It didn't last too long, but it was a booger.

Ideally, a dismounted cowhand under the threat of hail would tie his horse. But whether secured by limb or held by hand, the animal often broke free, as Alton Davis found out during a long-ago ordeal on the YO Ranch in the Texas Hill Country.

"An ol' boy and I was riding young horses when it come up a hailstorm," he narrated. "By gosh, we jumped off of our horses and tied them and got our saddles. There was a lot of ol' thick, heavy cedars there, but that ol' hail was big and it poured her out. It beat the limbs off trees and knocked big places on the saddles. Well, my horse stayed tied, but the other ol' boy didn't tie his very good. He broke loose. When it was over, I got on my horse and found his half a mile from where he broke loose."

Sometimes a lone cowboy was in for quite a walk after such a misfortune. Charlie Drennan, caught by surprise by an electrical storm and deluge of hail in 1935 on the 7D Ranch south of Sterling City, managed to yank his saddle off but didn't have time to worry about his horse. Releasing the animal, Drennan endured the onslaught by huddling under the saddle, then started off on foot for the ranch house. Less than a hundred yards into what would be a five-mile trudge, he found reason to be shaken—there

Charlie Drennan in 1991.

under a charred tree lay twenty-seven sheep killed by lightning.

Such occurrences gave cowhands cause for concern anytime they considered taking refuge under a tree. Hail could bruise and maim, but lightning, as too many case histories proved, could send a cowboy to an early grave.

Bolts From the Sky

When Walter Hoelscher was a greenhorn on a ranch near Olfen in the 1910s, his father gave him a bit of advice about lightning: "Get off a horse and get out in the open where there's no tree or nothing around. Because the first thing lightning will hit is a tree or a horse."

Indeed, with lightning prone to strike the tallest object in an area, a cowboy astride a horse was in real danger, especially on the plains or in a scrub brush country. Still, if he were driving cattle or riding pasture, there was only so much he could do.

Sometimes, if he anticipated soon enough, he might put spurs to his horse and try to outdistance the storm.

"I was out a half-mile from the [ranch] house one time and I looked up and saw a little ol' cloud," recalled Bill Townsend. "It wasn't but just as big as a saddle blanket against the sky. I tore out back to the house and lightning started just as I got there and shoved my horse in under a tree. When it was over—it didn't last ten minutes—I went up to the corral where I had a couple of colts. That lightning had struck and killed one of them."

If out-racing a storm was infeasible, a cowhand in broken country might look for a natural shelter such as a rock overhang, despite its own vulnerability to lightning. More often, all a cowboy could do was dismount and hope for the best, as Claude Owens did in Crockett County about 1920. He related:

"One evening, my brother and I were riding in the pasture and a little cloud come up. It got pretty close and had lots of lightning. We went down in a canyon and unsaddled our horses. We were just standing there holding our horses with our saddles over our head, and the lightning hit pretty close. We looked over there and saw some sotols that it had set afire."

Merely dismounting wasn't always enough, for unless a cowboy distanced himself from his horse, he was still a prime target for a strike, as fourteen-year-old Clarence Arrott learned in 1915. Helping hold a cattle herd in Brewster County, Arrott saw a thunderhead rising over the Chihuahuan Desert.

"It didn't look like it was going to be a very big one," he recalled. "But it went to raining, and one ol' boy crawled off and sat down under his horse, between his legs. His foot was sticking out, and lightning struck and knocked his boot heels into the ground and knocked the horse down. It just sort of stunned the cowhand a little bit, but they had to dig his boot heels out of the ground."

Although lightning was a threat from the time the first cowboy mounted up back in open-range days, the danger grew more serious with the advent of fences. Barbed wire was an excellent electrical conductor, and even if discharges weren't imminent, cowboys might see spectacular displays in stormy weather.

"I've been out when it seemed like the air was just full of electricity and you could see it on the fences," noted Green Mankin.

Sometimes the effect was eerie. Caught out after dark in an ominous storm in 1933 or 1934, Ted Laughlin and a fellow hand had to trail alongside a fence to navigate the Paul Horney Ranch north of Clovis, New Mexico. Laughlin recalled:

> That was in the dust bowl days, and in the evenings the dust would come in there and, hell, you flat couldn't see nothing. A particular man and I was riding along pretty close to a fence [within ten or twelve feet], and a cloud come up, and a dust storm too. Them horses couldn't even see one another; they'd just nicker. It was just as dark as it ever gets anywhere—no way you could see your hand in front of you. Ever' now and then lightning would hit that fence and you could see it just dance down that fence line. You could just see the fire fly down that top strand. It'd be real bright, just like fire, a light that'd go pretty fast right on down the fence. Now that's kind of scary business.

All too often, a fence's role in an electrical storm was anything but benign. The wire and posts were notorious for drawing lightning, and any livestock or cowhands caught alongside were in real peril. It was not unusual in a storm's aftermath for a line rider to find a grisly scene under the barbs.

"One time we had eighteen head of steers killed when [a bolt] hit a barbed wire fence," recalled Otis Coggins, who cowboyed in South Texas and the Trans-Pecos. "In a rainstorm, these cattle would drift against a fence, maybe a hundred head. And it'd hit that fence and when it was all over with, there might be eighteen to twenty head laying there dead."

Almost every cowboy of the fenced era could tell a similar story. Max Reed, for example, once rode upon a pile of dead cattle bearing the Scharbauer brand after a seemingly innocuous rainstorm.

"It kinda started a little ol' shower out of the east and they'd backed up against a barbed wire fence that was running north and south," he related. "And somewhere up and down the line, lightning must have hit that fence, because it killed all fourteen of them ol' cows standing there."

Often, the carcasses left no doubt that the animals had met with a swift and certain end. Crockett County cowhand Ted Powers, riding across a lightning-felled bull in the pasture, found its hooves "black as coal on the bottom, like charcoal."

With fences often dictating the course of a roundup or cattle drive, cowboys all too frequently found themselves courting the gravedigger. In 1931 Jack Cauble counted himself lucky to be on drag on a drive in New Mexico. Pushing cattle down a fence line on the Park Springs Ranch between Santa Rosa and Las Vegas, he saw a bolt of lightning kill two of the animals.

Lee Brice had his own narrow escape east of Plains about 1929. Helping two other hands drive 200 cattle north along a fence marking the Texas-New Mexico line, Brice pulled rein hard when a lethal bolt dropped a steer only fifty yards away.

Lee Brice on the Jake McClure Ranch near Lovington, New Mexico, in the 1930s. (courtesy, Lee Brice)

"That lightning would go right down their leg and into the ground and kill 'em," he noted.

Any time a tree loomed over a stretch of barbed wire, the danger was magnified. S. M. "Si" Loeffler, who hired on with the Centennial Spring Ranch near Mason in 1917, recalled:

"We were rounding up cattle one time and it blew up a thunderstorm and the durndest lightning and thunder.

47

This particular steer, with the bunch we were driving, was across the fence trying to get to the herd. The lightning hit the top of a big live oak tree, ran right down the trunk, and uprooted two big roots [about a foot apart]. It followed those roots and hit that fence about twenty feet away. Like fire as big as my finger, it ran on down that fence about 100 feet. When it got to the steer, it jumped over and killed him, broke every bone in him."

Even in the absence of a nearby fence or tree, the standard tools of a cowboy's trade could make things chancy in a thunderstorm. Spurs, which some cowhands feared would attract lightning, could be shed easily, but a saddle was a different matter.

"They always told us not to use iron stirrups on your saddle and said, 'If you got a silver horn, take and wrap it with something,'" recalled Willard Renfro, who began cowboying in the 1910s.

Charlie Cone, a cowhand in the Panhandle and eastern New Mexico, took the latter advice to heart. "When we was out at night like that standing guard," he related, "a lot of us had those silver-horned saddles, and we'd always put our glove over that saddle horn and just cover it up."

Still, every cowhand knew that punching cattle when lightning rent the sky was risky business, a fact reinforced by every near-miss. Remembered Panhandle cowboy Frank Yeary:

"I was down there at that Swenson [SMS] outfit one time and we'd worked all day rounding up, and we'd been wet five or six times. When we got through we started to the holding pasture with the cut—didn't lack half a mile being there—and I was in the point. It come a keen clap of thunder and lightning and killed the two lead cattle, and I just turned around and headed to the wagon. Ever' cowboy I had on the outfit followed me."

Frank Yeary in 1989.

Even a dependable horse reacted strongly to a nearby strike, while a bronc might test even the most experienced hand. "Lightning would hit close to a horse and it'd pop and splatter," noted Renfro. "Damn, those horses would jump and kick, and they'd try to run away from you."

If the lightning came closer, the difference between life and death sometimes was no greater than the breadth of a horse hair, as Charles K. Smith found out just after World War I on the Charco de los Marinos Ranch north of Marfa.

"My brother [Tyrrel] and I were rounding up and it came up a lightning storm," he recalled. "The herd was nervous, and we were holding it and circling it, and we were coming around to meet each other. And when we were about forty or fifty feet apart, lightning hit the ground right halfway between us and knocked my horse to his knees. I stayed in the saddle, but that's the worst scared I ever was."

Thomas Henderson, helping drive 600 head of cattle from Silver Lake in the Big Bend north to Marathon in 1925 or 1926, shared the same terrible dread. Soaking wet after a downpour, Henderson found the trail marked by the iron posts of a telephone line dating to the U.S. Army's campaign against Pancho Villa. As he brought up the drags, Henderson noted the way the desert fell away abruptly on the herd's flank. It dropped thirty feet or more, all the way to the rocky bed of Reynolds Creek.

About him, lightning was strafing the countryside, finding ridges and crags, sotol and yucca. Watching with increasing anxiety, he was momentarily blinded by a nearby bolt that blew a scrub mesquite "all to hell."

Still, he steadied his six-year-old gelding "Boots" and kept the drags in check. Suddenly, almost in his face, an iron post took a wicked hit from the clouds.

"It looked like that post jumped ten feet high," related Henderson. "That ol' horse went down on his knees and scared the hell out of me. I could've fell over his head if I hadn't been paying attention. He wobbled around and I didn't know whether to get off or not. I thought I might have to run, so I didn't. That horse couldn't run anyway; he was pretty addled. He staggered around a little bit and got up."

Henderson wasn't alone in his plight. The other drovers—two on flank, another on drag—were as shaken as he, but they held their positions in fear of a stampede. The cattle, however, were as dazed as the horses.

"It knocked seven or eight cows down there in front of me," said Henderson. "They got up and staggered around and I was afraid they were going to fall off that bluff, but they didn't ever run."

With the herd under control, Henderson realized the odd odor in the air. "You could smell that lightning," he recalled, "a sulfuric odor, just like somebody'd set sulphur afire. I'd been wet all over, plum' to the bone, and it kind of dried me off."

Sometimes the diffusing currents did more than stun a cowhand's horse and make the air reek.

"In Concho County about 1926, I was just riding in the pasture and had a sheep dog," remembered Orval Sparks. "It come up a cloud and went to raining, and I put on my slicker. This dog got closer and closer to the horse. It come a clap of thunder and I saw the lightning hit right close to the dog, about twenty feet to the side of me. I felt the shock, just like you were struck all over your body with pins. My horse run and tried to throw me, but along about then I was an awful good rider."

The dog escaped injury, but Sparks was convinced that the animal's role in the incident was pivotal. "Lots of people think it's an old wives' tale that dogs draw lightning," he observed, "but they *definitely* draw lightning—it happened to me."

Sam Hutchison, a foreman for a ranch near Brackettville, was one of the few riders to walk away after a direct strike. Driving three cows through a long-ago storm, he somehow survived a bolt that not only killed his horse and two of the cattle, but burned a hole the size of a silver dollar through the seat of his saddle.

All too often, though, a lightning strike meant tragedy, with whimsical fate and the inscrutable ways of nature deciding the victim. Bill Shields, who worked for the Lee Bivins outfit in Texas and New Mexico, recalled a couple of fellow hands who rode up to a gate in a mid-1920s storm. Aware of the danger the fence posed, the two men held rein and argued about which of them would open it. Finally one cowboy surrendered and climbed off his horse. Just as he reached the gate, lightning struck and killed the man who had stayed mounted.

Death, whether by lightning or vicious bronc or crazed steer, was something nearly all cowhands had seen. If they didn't understand it, they at least accepted it as the natural order of things. But when devil's fire swooped down out of a stormy sky and danced before their very eyes, even the most stoic hands often had to get a grip on themselves.

St. Elmo's Fire

From the time the flinty hooves of the longhorn first cut a cattle trail out of Texas, bound for points east, west, or north, one particular phenomenon invariably sent a chill down a cowboy's spine. Spooky even to a person versed in nature, St. Elmo's fire (known simply as lightning to cowhands) was a rare, luminous display of electricity that could send tongues of flame leaping from the horns of a storm-boogered herd.

Sometimes it came on the heels of a radiant aura that settled on the ground and crept along like a fiend.

"It'll scare the hell out of you," said Weir Hall, who witnessed the effect on a cattle drive in northern Oklahoma in 1950. "This was in the middle of the day, about one or two o'clock, and it was real hot. Then that came in kind of green, rolling on the ground like a fog. When it started, it was sun a-shinin', then that glowing fog clouded over. The cattle won't move. They just stand there and bawl. The lightning just kind of flutters on them like a ball of fire, rolling down their necks and the points of their ears. Everything turns green, but that lightning will look like a fire."

Louis Baker, making a morning roundup drive in Oklahoma in 1918, witnessed a similar occurrence.

"That was one time I was really, really scared," he noted. "I was going under a railroad bridge with them cattle when it come up a little lightning spell. The lightning up there in that country didn't seem to be like the lightning is here [in Texas]. It'd hit and just run straight through there level instead of coming straight down. You could see that tipping off of them cattle's horns. Man, I had to get out of there."

Oklahoma and the South Plains seemed prone to nurturing uncanny spectacles. Gid Reding, who cowboyed throughout the West and once rode horseback from the Mexico border to Montana, saw ball lightning nowhere but the Cimarron and Canadian River country.

"When smart alecks tell you there's not any ball lightning, they don't know what they're talking about," he observed. "When the weather gets right, it'll hit and just bounce along several hundred yards."

More commonly in Texas and New Mexico, St. Elmo's fire seemed to flare suddenly, without a luminous fog or ball lightning to presage it. Still, a cowhand found plenty to be uneasy about, for it generally occurred only in stormy weather when the air was loaded with electricity.

"It'd light up the whole herd just dancing around on their horns," said Otis Coggins, an eyewitness to the wonder. "It'd kind of run down the backbone of the cattle and go out on their horns. It happened often if you was on guard and had a thunderstorm. The worst part would be before the rain started, [when there was] thunder and flashing."

One night about 1925, fifteen-year-old Ralph Davis found himself facing not only a storm, but 750 head of spooked Herefords on a drive with nine other hands from near Big Spring to San Angelo. He recalled:

"We had 'em throwed in a corner, then it come up a little ol' cloud, started showering and thundering. [The boss] kicked us ever' one out [of camp] and made us stand guard, keep 'em in. Everybody had horned cattle so they could fight the coyotes off their calves, and ever' once in a while you could see that lightning jump through these old cow's horns, just pop. That's when they're restless. It looked like

Ralph Davis at age 16.
(courtesy, Ralph Davis)

a spark plug fire, only bigger, and it'd maybe jump off this ol' cow's horns and just sorta go up so high and just go out [vanish]."

In the fall of 1930, Slim Vines observed the phenomenon while riding guard over 1,300 mixed cattle on the Texas South Plains.

"You could see that electricity just waving in every direction all over the cattle at night," he remembered. "Seemed like it'd jump from their horns more than any other place. It might come off their back, but it'd go directly to the horns. It'd be various colors, purple and green and blue mixed in with the color of lightning. It'd jump from one cow's horns to another's if they got a little bit close. And it was just a continuous popping, a snapping, all over the herd, just like an electrical wire shorting out."

Such a dynamic example of St. Elmo's fire, with a soundtrack like the chorus of a thousand cicadas or the crackle of a range fire, meant an especially intense electric field surrounded the horns. Still, to a cowboy battling an ominous storm and a herd ready to bolt, understanding the rarity would have done little to comfort him. Such was the case with Tom Duncan in Mason County in the early 1930s.

"It looked like we was gonna get blowed away," he related. "It come up a storm, rained, hailed, wind blew. That lightning just danced around all over the herd like a ball of fire, just real bright. But we held the cattle together."

Sometimes St. Elmo's fire could fascinate as well as unnerve, due in part to its myriad colors.

"That is a frightening and interesting experience, to see it playing off a cow's horns," said Olan George, who twice observed the phenomenon on the Hood Mendel spread near Fort Stockton in the mid-1920s. On one particular night, as he rode guard around 500 cattle ablaze in St. Elmo's fire, he marveled at its strange appeal even while shrinking from it.

"It's a beautiful sight," he recalled. "It just looks like a fire floating, just kind of a wave, blue and then the red color, and silver or the color of lightning. And the cattle will sling their heads and blow, and that's when there's the danger of a stampede."

The threat of stampede, it seems, was due less to St. Elmo's fire than to the weather conditions that bred the curiosity.

"The cattle would be a-millin' if it was a dark night and lightning," remembered Panhandle cowboy Tom Blasingame, who rode guard under such conditions. "Generally, you'd be a-runnin'; you'd be a-worryin' about whether you was on the outside of all the cattle, whether you was leaving cattle to your left. But I could see that lightning play on the tips of my horse's ears, red like fire."

It was especially startling for a cowboy to find the ghostly flames so near, but some riders experienced it even more intimately.

"I've seen the ball of fire run down my horse's neck and, when it'd get to your saddle horn, just split and go off on each side," recalled Frank Yeary.

Mysterious and intimidating, the hellish apparition drove some cowboys to consider immediate action.

"I thought, my God, I got a six-shooter—they said the old-timers throwed their gun away; I ain't gonna throw MINE away!" recalled Thomas Henderson, who once found his horse's mane and ears enveloped.

Although a horse seemed not to notice the aura, some cowhands could barely resist the temptation to pass a trembling hand through it.

"I noticed it on my horse, all over him," said Wier Hall of his 1950 experience in Oklahoma. "It'd just go right down him. It looked like you could just reach out and pick it off of his ears. The points of his ears would just glow like a light."

Sometimes the fire would torch a metal saddle horn or, at its most extreme, find an anxious cowboy's hat brim or even wreathe his person.

"I've seen it play on cowboy's spurs—in fact, it's played on mine," said Ted Powers, who was a hand on the T. A. Kincaid spread near Ozona in 1925. "This ol' boy at Kincaid's, Ernest Hensley, lightning was playing on all his spur rowels. And he pulled his spurs off and rode off and left 'em. He went back a few days later to find 'em and he never did."

Maybe a drover didn't know what to make of St. Elmo's fire, but he knew well the danger of lightning and stampede—insight that compelled Douglas Poage and J. R. "Jim" Stroup to abandon glowing herds in the 1920s and ride hard for camp.

Poage's herd was the larger, 1,100 cows, and when a storm blew in one night between Lubbock and Midland, every cowhand in the outfit rode out to hold the boogered animals.

"It was raining hard and lightning," recalled Poage. "There was just a streak of fire jumping from horn to horn. Cattle was trying to run and we was trying to hold them. But we couldn't and the boss said, 'Just turn 'em loose.' So we went to the wagon."

Remarkably, the bolting cattle remained bunched, and the next morning the drovers quickly had the animals rounded up and pointed down-trail.

J. R. "Jim" Stroup in 1989.

The Stroup outfit, driving 150 to 200 head across the Panhandle from Briscoe County to Floydada, was not so lucky.

"One night a cloud caught us, and that was the worst electric storm I was ever out in on a horse with cattle," remembered Stroup. "We was trying to hold them close to a barbed wire fence. You could see electricity on the hair of the cows' backs, and it'd just jump from horn to horn. My dad finally found me [around the herd]. He said 'Let 'em go! Let 'em go!' And they *did* go. The rest of us spent the next day gathering them up, and Dad spent the next day trying to pay guys off for damage they done."

Few drovers, Poage and Stroup included, had much stomach for deserting a herd. Indeed, if a cowhand had a real choice, he usually would stick with a bunch of bony cattle all the way to hell. All too often, however, his admirable loyalty only sentenced him to a wild ride amid the clashing horns of a thousand beeves stampeding straight for a midnight grave.

Pummeling
Hooves

With nostrils flaring and hooves thundering, they charged into the night—hundreds of beeves suddenly transformed into a single destructive force bent on trampling anything in its path.

To a cowboy, it was a "stom-peed," and of all situations he faced in a life in the saddle, nothing else could compare for sheer fury and awesome power. A bolting herd was stupendous and dramatic, frightening and dangerous, and it tested a cowboy's skill and mettle to the utmost.

"If you'd run out in front of 'em," said drover W. R. Green, "they'd run over you, kill you and your horse too."

In the heyday of the great cattle trails of legend, when a Texas cowboy might spend months pushing longhorns up the Pecos or elsewhere, stampedes were most common early in a drive, before a herd was "trail-broke." By the 1900s, with railroad shipping points springing up across the Southwest, epic drives were all but a memory. For a cowhand, it was a development both welcome and ominous, for the fact that a drive required only a few days meant that the unseasoned animals were a real threat to "head for the high-lonesome" every minute a drover held position around a herd.

Like the early free-ranging longhorns, which might shy at their own shadows, some twentieth-century cattle seemed to be just waiting for an excuse to run. Steers and other "dry stock" were the worst offenders, but even the most docile animals could go on a rampage at literally the drop of a hat.

"When gentle cattle get scared, they're crazier than wild cattle," noted cowhand Green Mankin.

Inexperience on the part of drovers, such as failing to recognize especially restless beeves, could hasten a stampede, but there was only so much that even a veteran outfit could do. In driving, the boss could properly position riders at point, swing, and drag, and when holding a herd overnight, he could send out a prudent number of hands (every man in the outfit if conditions warranted) to ride guard in shifts and try to reassure the cattle. A wise boss also realized that most stampedes came after 10 P.M., with the threat intensifying with the toll of midnight and extending halfway to dawn. Still, he could only watch and wait unless the cattle were milling, in which case he might keep the fitful animals circling to spend their nervous energy. Meanwhile, a few hundred yards away at the chuck wagon, any unneeded cowboys would be sprawled out fully dressed in their bedrolls trying to catch some shut-eye, their hats and boots at arm's reach and their saddled horses staked nearby for use at a moment's notice. All too often, however, the transition from sleep to wakefulness for even a top hand came unexpectedly, triggered by the shrill cry of *stampede!*

Holding a herd near Beal's Creek on the Spade Ranch in the late 1920s or early 1930s. (courtesy, Fred McClellan)

Big Bend cowboy Thomas Henderson learned at an early age the frenzy at camp that usually followed. Six years old and on a fifty-mile drive from Silver Lake Ranch to Marathon in the fall of 1914, he watched the drovers throw a herd of 450 to 500 sore-footed steers up against a rocky hill at sundown. With the coming of night, his father tucked him in his bedroll against the chill of a steady rain. Waiting for his father to join him in repose, the boy saw him take measures that reflected his trail wisdom—he rested his pillow on a coil of rope leading to his night horse, whose stirrings could alert him to trouble.

Far into the night, the sleeping boy's first inkling that a vicious clap of thunder had started the cattle running came with his father's cry: "Boys, let's go get 'em!"

"He hollered about twice," recalled the younger Henderson, "and you could hear those ol' boys' spurs a-rattlin', pulling on their old wet boots and covering up their beds, getting their horses. You'd be surprised at how those ol' guys would wake up just like that and know what was going on. Papa told me to get up and get in the wagon, up on the wagon sheet. That wagon sheet was four feet long and roomy enough for me to lay down on. He told me he didn't know where those cattle was going, but if that stompede come by, he didn't want them to catch me in bed. For two or three weeks at a time, I wouldn't take my clothes off, so all I had to do was pull on my boots and my hat. It was dark and raining and thundering; I couldn't see anything. But they all went to the herd, fast as they could."

Willard Renfro was also a young witness to the fuss a stampede could cause in a trail drive camp. Unrolling his bedding near the Llano River on an eighty-mile push across the Hill Country in the early 1920s, he listened attentively to trail boss Alvin Neal's concerns for their 350 spayed heifers and handful of longhorn steers.

"Now, I want you boys to get up a good gentle horse, night horse, and leave him saddled," Neal told the drovers. "These cattle are pretty restless and they'll probably break out if the least little thing moves."

Only fourteen or so, Renfro lay wide-eyed in his bedroll on into hard dark, anticipation and excitement filling him. Then came sudden thunder, despite a sky jeweled with stars.

"Get your horses, boys!" cried Neal. "Got to ride *now!*"

Reaching for his boots, Renfro readied to join the other drovers, only to whirl at the boss's voice. "You stay here at the wagon!" Neal ordered.

Primed for the chase, the young cowhand obeyed only reluctantly.

"Made me mad," Renfro recalled. "I wanted to go too, but it was a good thing I didn't, 'cause they rode all night. You could hear everybody running. Horses was stumbling around. And the herd got away from us."

Willard Renfro in 1990.

When beeves broke and ran, the scene around camp was frantic enough, but no one knew the fever of a stampede's outburst better than the hands who rode guard, for they were astride horses at the very fringe of the bolting cattle.

"They'd throw their tails over their backs, *ka-bloom!*" said veteran herder Shorty Northcutt.

"They're just like a bunch of quail flying—it'll just happen all at once," noted Otis Coggins, who lived through stampedes on both sides of the Rio Grande. "Some might get cut off in the side or behind, but they'd generally always follow one another, just all stay in a bunch."

Even if the animals were lying down and seemingly at ease, experienced guards kept in mind a herd's unpredictability.

"Everything would be just as quiet as it could be," said Slim Vines, "and before you could snap your fingers, ever' animal in that herd would be on its feet. And there's no way of keeping 'em from running."

"When one jumps they all jump, and all of a sudden they're gone," noted Si Loeffler. "And you'd better not be in their way, because they'll run smack-dab over you."

"You can't imagine," added Green Mankin, "how quick them cattle could disappear."

Fred McClellan, riding guard over 2,000 yearlings near Colorado City one day about 1934, learned for himself just how swiftly a calm herd could go mad. "Something boogered 'em," he recalled, "and them things got on their feet so damned quick I never saw it. I don't know how they do it. They run and just got crazy."

The din of a herd stampeding at twenty-five to thirty miles per hour was incredible, especially to a rider in its midst. Many cowhands compared it to a thunderstorm or to the clamor under a trestle when a freight train barreled over, while a few old-time drovers could still hear the bedlam across three-quarters of a century.

"You take 2,000 head of two-year-old steers, full of life and restless, and when they break to run, now they're *running*," noted Tom Blasingame, who forked his share of horses around skittish herds. "You can hear that roaring. Them ol' horses would just go wild, you know. They'd jump and run same time the cattle would. How they knew it, I don't know. You could feel their heart a-beatin' against your leg."

Tom Blasingame in his early years as a cowboy. (courtesy, *Persimmon Hill Magazine*)

When the chase was on through the choking dust, a cowboy needed a superb horse, for on the animal rested not only the fate of the herd, but his very life, especially in a night stampede. Charging through impenetrable dark at thirty miles per hour, passing one cow brute after another in pursuit of the leaders, he could only hang on and trust in his gelding's innate night vision and balance to save him from a sudden fall.

"If you didn't have a good night horse you might get killed pretty easy," said Blasingame. "They was pretty wise, you know, sure-footed. That's all we used 'em for, to stand guard on."

Still, in the mad race through the gloom, even the best horse could land a cowboy in a shallow grave.

"You couldn't see the bushes and brush and holes," said Slim Vines. "Used to be lots of rats in this [West Texas] country that dug a hole out and had a great big perforated mound there. A horse that runs over that at night, he's gonna go down to his belly. And there's lot of badgers, and they'd dig a big ol' hole and it goes almost straight down. A horse steps in that, he'll go plumb up to his knees."

The danger was compounded by the surging herd at a rider's side, for it was a storming mass of wild-eyed devils that threatened to run all the way to doomsday.

"They'll run like hell and they'll run over you too, if you ain't careful," said drover Buck Murrah.

Asking his horse for more than it had to give, a dedicated cowboy nevertheless clung to their flank, his eyes fixed on the hidden front runners that led the charge through splintering brush and popping strands of barbed wire. But even as he neared point, trouble probably brewed behind, for the herd often splintered on swing or drag, as a few cattle "ducked out" and others followed their lead.

"If you hadn't got enough help, you'll get to losing a lot of your cattle," noted Frank Derrick of Clarendon. "You're way up there where you can't take care of both bunches."

Maynard "Fish" Wilson, riding in a number of JA stampedes in the Panhandle, learned to anticipate the problem. "I'd be back on drag," he recalled. "They said when something like that happens, make the drag come on. That was one rule they give me over there—if they run, make them others come on."

How far a boogered herd would stampede varied. Rarely, resting cattle might jump to their feet and wheel in the same direction, only to hold their ground. Usually, though, their sudden stirring was in prelude to a run that carried them from a few hundred yards to several miles, depending on the make-up of the herd and the success of the pursuing cowboys. Cows with calves, for example, sometimes ran only a short distance before stopping to seek their young. Mature steers, meanwhile, might virtually wear down a horse before yielding. Often bearing back toward their home range, in first a crazed run and then a fast walk, the beeves might drift fifteen miles from midnight till dawn. Unchecked runaways could actually run themselves to death, or meet the fate that befell scores of three-year-old Matador steers near Channing about 1940.

"We had 4,000 of 'em in a small pasture," recalled John Stevens, a division manager for the Matador at the time. "We was going to ship 'em by rail and they ran in the night. They piled up in the head of a canyon and killed ninety of 'em. All the others ran over 'em and they smothered down under there."

If disaster didn't befall a herd beforehand, the advance cowboy had a single responsibility as he finally gained point—to turn the leaders by whatever means possible and start the herd circling.

"You can't stop 'em as long as they're running straight," said Green Mankin. "You can just run and try with a hat or something to get 'em to giving."

"You'd have your jacket off and just a-hollerin' and shakin' it, trying to get the lead steers to turn," said Otis Coggins. "If it was a rainstorm that stompeded 'em, you'd pull your slicker off and use it."

Riding under the whip alongside 1,120 rampaging beeves near Barnhart about 1932, Louis Baker drew upon another trick of the trade: "First thing you'd do, you'd reach down and grab your rope, use the coil and whip your leggings and holler to turn 'em."

Famed cowman Charles Goodnight, who drove cattle up stretches of the Goodnight-Loving Trail for nine years, believed a herd would veer and circle only clockwise. Such assertions led Texas cowhand Gaston Boykin to muse whether a milling herd's bent for a certain direction, like that of a tornado or draining water, depended on its position on the rotating Earth. "Cattle always turn to the right, they claim, in this country," said Boykin. "I've always wondered if down south, the other side of the equator, if they turn to the left."

Other Southwestern drovers, reflecting on their own experiences, weren't so sure about Goodnight's claim, instead maintaining that each stampede was a highly individualized event. A mill's direction, they said, could be dictated by the terrain, vegetation, and weather, and by how those factors affected cowboys in their charge up the flanks.

"It seems like we always pushed 'em to the left," said Ralph Davis. "But I think it's according to them cowboys, whichever side they come up and went to pushing 'em around and around."

In fact, Frank Derrick learned to prefer a mill direction contrary to the course noted by Goodnight. "Most of the time when you'd have a run that a-way," he noted, "if you'd go counterclockwise, it'd seem like you'd have better control over 'em than if you'd go clockwise."

With any attempt at communication lost in the roar and blinding dust (if not the hard dark), a lot of intuitive teamwork was necessary to start the cattle circling.

"If they was circling to the left, the fellows on that side would kinda drop back to give room to circle 'em," noted Coggins.

A cowboy caught on the wrong side of a veering herd sometimes took reckless action in the face of thousands of pummeling hooves. "You might ride *through* the herd and get on the other side and help bring 'em back around," said Slim Vines.

When there were no longer any cowboys to inhibit the course of the leaders, the point riders forced their horses ever closer, inducing the beeves to swerve more and more dramatically.

"You'd just go to circling," explained Ralph Davis. "Every time you'd come around, you'd make the circle a little shorter."

For drover Fish Wilson, a skittish herd bound for Ashtola in 1940 became a study in technique. "In four or five miles time, I guess they run four or five times," he remembered. "They'd break to run and them ol' boys would just stay with 'em and they'd bring 'em around and run 'em into theirself."

The result, in any stampede, was inevitable. "Finally they just jam up," said Ted Powers.

For an alkali-caked cowboy fresh out of a backsliding Christian's prayers, the ensuing mill was a welcome sight.

"If you ever got 'em to milling," said Otis Coggins, "you could kinda settle 'em down and hold 'em." Still, he recognized the potential for more trouble, for the shaken animals sometimes would continue to mill until daybreak as they "bawled and raised sand."

Twelve-year-old Lewis Doran, one of seven drovers in charge of 500 longhorn cows near Eden one night in 1919, quickly earned his spurs in coping with ornery cattle both during and after a run. He recalled:

> We were sitting out there on horses, and boy, here they come towards us, just a-flyin'. This ol' boss told us right quick to get in front of 'em, circle 'em. So we just circled the lead cattle back to the right and let 'em come on around. They made about three runs, around and around. Got 'em slowed down, got 'em stopped, but all night those cattle wouldn't lay down—they'd stand up there and bawl

and wanted to walk. We left a couple of extra men out there with 'em that night; I think there was five of us standing at one time.

Lewis Doran in 1990.

Daybreak always brought its own concerns, for only then could the trail boss count his losses. "Sometimes you'd lose a hundred head," noted Otis Coggins. "There'd be a bunch of boys start on their trail and trail 'em up, and we'd get 'em back to the herd."

After spending hours or days getting the animals back in one drove, more work remained—cutting out strays. In a barbed wire West, it was accepted practice to lay a hindering fence down momentarily and point a drove across range pastured by other cattle. In the excitement of a stampede, the native stock often joined the runaways.

A fence itself could pose a problem in the wake of a run, for broken wire and splintered posts could litter the countryside. If drovers couldn't patch it with existing materials or chuck wagon supplies, they might spend another day or two rounding up the necessary items and making repairs.

Often the situation forced cowboys to become adept at digging postholes. Steve Armentrout, who helped drive 1,700 Howard Draw steers to Barnhart in the early 1930s, remembered the beeves flattening so many fences that "we had to have a fencing crew to follow 'em. I don't know how many trips them boys had to make back to town and get more wire."

A fence leveled by stampede was so commonplace that ranches sometimes resigned themselves to the calamity. A Crockett County ranch hand, finding several downed fences after a passing drove of 800 steers stampeded near Live Oak Creek in the 1920s, shrugged off drover Bud Mayes' offer to do the honorable thing.

"In those days," recalled Mayes, "it wasn't much job to fix back or tear down those ol' barbed wire fences. We told the ol' boy we'd come back soon as we turned those cattle loose [at a nearby ranch] and help him fix 'em up. 'Aw, naw,' he says, 'just leave 'em down. They'll run over and knock more down anyway.'"

And run they would, for reasons big and small and beyond the ken of even the most astute cowhand.

What Made 'Em Run

Only after a stampeding herd was in a mill might a trail boss twist around in the saddle, look back through the settling dust, and consider what had boogered the animals. Storms, he couldn't control, but imprudent acts on the part of his hands were another matter. Certainly, in no other phase of a cowhand's job could inexperience sow the seeds of such catastrophe, and some cowmen were always ready to rush to judgment.

"A stompede's usually caused by somebody that don't know what they're doing," said Leonard Proctor.

Steve Armentrout, riding swing on a herd of 1,700 grown steers west of Ozona in the early 1930s, witnessed a classic example of disaster stemming from a drover's ill-advised deed. As the cattle ambled up into a gap through rugged hills, one cowboy's horse shied at the staccato of a rattler. Dismounting, the man unwisely drew a small-caliber pistol and took aim.

"He shot that thing, and boy, them cattle was gone," remembered Armentrout. "I spurred my horse right on up past him; I saw they was gonna have trouble up in front. I went on up there and those cattle went over that hill. The herd was stringing out faster all the time. We finally milled 'em around down in a flat."

Less dramatic in his approach but just as foolish was a greenhorn charged with guarding 600 steers on a sunny flat near the stock pens in Barnhart in 1925. Unaccountably off his horse, he noticed a few nearby steers beginning to stray. Instead of mounting up and turning the beeves like a cowboy, he chose the lazy course of action—he picked up a tow sack of tin cans and threw it in their path.

"Man, you talk about leaving there; those cattle *left* there," recalled Ted Powers, who was at the stock pens at the time. "Somebody said, 'Your steers are running!' We saw 'em and we jumped on our horses and took after 'em. They hit a horse pasture fence and just flattened it, and run on across the pasture and flattened it going out on the other side. We finally got 'em in a mill."

Often, a trail boss charged the youngest cowboy with wrangling horses, a job in which a thorough knowledge of the cow brute wasn't so vital. Still, horse "jingling" required a certain measure of common sense—a commodity lacking in one greenhorn on a drive from a ranch near Big Lake to Coke County in 1926.

Reaching a brushy prong of the Concho River late one day, the outfit turned 2,200 troublesome beeves into a mile-square trap. Night passed without incident, but as soon as day broke, pandemonium erupted.

"That danged 'ol city boy went out there wrangling horses and squalled right loud, and those cattle went over the fence in every direction," recalled drover Gid Reding. "We stayed there three days and finally left about seventy head in that brush."

Even a mere moment of carelessness could give rise to trouble. As dark fell over camp one night on the east-bearing trail to Barnhart, Armentrout whirled as a drover clumsily dropped a skillet. "You can imagine what kind of racket *that* made," recalled Armentrout. No sooner had the skillet hit the chuck box than the cattle were up and running, taking a fence with them.

Sometimes the most innocuous of mistakes could spur a herd into sudden flight. Just before daybreak one chilly morning in the 1920s, Bud Mayes rode out from camp to stand guard over 700 to 800 restless animals two miles east of Rankin. "They'd walked all night long and they was dry for water and hungry and tired," recalled Mayes.

Bud Mayes in 1990.

In his slow circle about the herd, Mayes met up with approaching guard Jimmy O'Brien, an older hand who had spent much of the night astride a horse. "The old man smoked one Durham cigarette right after another," remembered Mayes.

As Mayes peered at the old cowhand through the dark, he found him humped up, shivering from the cold and the need for a smoke.

"Bud," said O'Brien with a quake in his voice, "I'm just dying for a cigarette and I can't roll one, it's dark. I've just gotta have a cigarette now, that's all there are to it."

Fresh from a warm bed, Mayes took pity on the old man. "Oh well," he said, "give me your tobacco and I'll go out there and see if I can get one a-goin'."

Wise to the ways of a skittish herd, Mayes took O'Brien's sack of tobacco and rode away from the herd. Related Mayes:

> I went off about a hundred yards out there and got down and rolled a cigarette for the old man, and then just struck a match on my stirrup. *Od-durn!* When that flash took that light, it scared these cattle and away they went. I crawled on my horse and took out in the lead of 'em and kept a-hollerin' and raising Cain. They run about a mile, I guess, tore down two or three fences and run over and broke one of 'em's legs.

It wasn't the only time the strike of a match kindled such fury.

"We used to run lots of cattle out of the northern part of Coahuila, Mexico, way back before that revolution," recalled Big Bend cowboy Francis Rooney, who was born in

1899. "We'd cross 'em over [the Rio Grande] and bring 'em to Marathon to the railroad. Along about 1912 I was standing guard at night about twenty-five miles southwest of Marathon. We had about 1,800 big steers. Some ol' boy lit a match to see what time it was, and it was too bad—they'd all taken off."

Even if cattle seemingly were at ease, the sudden flash could wreak havoc with the night. Clarence Arrott, part of an outfit holding a herd near Ozona about 1915, witnessed an unsuspecting guard lighting a smoke as the animals sprawled contentedly in the dark.

"They jumped up and pulled out," recalled Arrott, who immediately gave chase. Even so, the herd disappeared into the night, forcing the drovers to make an exhaustive roundup the next day.

For the relatively few drovers who didn't smoke or carry a pocket watch, the wisdom of whether or not to strike a match wasn't a consideration. Still, like all cowboys, they made their living astride a cow pony, an often unpredictable animal that demanded everything a man had in the way of anticipation and horse savvy. Around a nervous herd, even the simple act of dismounting could have dire consequences.

"Pretty near anytime you get off a horse and he's kinda sweaty and his back's burning, why, he'll shake his saddle," noted Otis Coggins. "Dat-gum, that'd stompede a herd quicker than anything. You just couldn't get off your horse."

Knowing when and where to dismount was one thing, but even a top hand was powerless when a bronc decided to shake itself ("just like a dog," said Mayes) with a rider astride. The only thing he could do was grit his teeth for a wild chase through the billowing dust.

Helping drive 300 peaceful heifers up a long draw in the Barnhart region about 1932, Louis Baker studied fellow drover Gene Linthecum just moments before the dust rose in a fury. "His horse was trailing along and just stopped and shook," recalled Baker. "When it did, it shook that saddle. Boy, every cow hit the ground running. They ran two miles before we had 'em settled down."

Similarly, the best of riders could only tense and wait for the roar of hooves if their horses stumbled noisily. But when it came to controlling a troublesome bronc, even a young cowboy knew there'd be hell to pay if he didn't go light with the spurs around a restless herd.

Riding drag on a bronc one day, Marvin Hooper noticed that the hackamore had worked back on the animal's neck. "I reached over to move that hackamore," recalled Hooper. "Boy, when I did, he went to bucking. I got a little overbalanced, but I sort of straightened up and I went to spurring him. I rode him, all right, but them cattle had just went everywhere. Boy, I mean we scattered 'em all over the country."

After it was all over, the trail boss, who believed Hooper had provoked the bronc, gathered his hands for a lecture on the overzealous use of spurs. "Boys," he said, "don't *ever* hang 'em in to a bronc behind a bunch of calves."

"I didn't hang 'em in to that horse," spoke up Hooper, who had applied spurs only after the animal had begun to pitch. "He just fell in two and went to bucking."

At times, a horse needed only to nicker to set off a herd, as Charlie Cone learned about 1924 after bedding down 300 Hereford steers in a pasture corner near Caprock, New Mexico. "Along after supper, I rode off down there to see how they was doing," remembered Cone.

There was an ol' pony loose down there some-where, and he nickered. When he did, the ol' pony I was riding nickered back. Every steer in that bunch jumped up, just stopped for a second, then broke and run. They made a circle around up through there and run over and tore down a half-mile of fence. We run for about two miles before we got ahead of 'em and got 'em slowed down.

Sometimes cattle bolted for purely topographic rea-sons. When trailing down a steep slope, for example, they might yield to the tug of gravity, as was the case with 400 winter calves near Quitaque in 1941.

"We was driving 'em off the caprock and didn't have nobody in the lead," remembered Troy "Jones" Taylor. "They just didn't have nobody to hold 'em up, and they started down that hill and just started running on us. They got away and run about a couple of miles. I finally managed to get in the lead and keep these other boys from holler-ing."

Once a herd broke into a downhill run, the action was fast and furious, and any cowboy with the gumption to ride for the lead faced added danger.

Rounding up in a pasture ten miles south of Vancourt about 1934, Hewitt Alexander and the wagon boss briefly held 300 Hereford steers on the point of a big hill. "We was waiting for the other two cowboys to get there," Alexander recalled.

Suddenly, without apparent provocation, the steers whirled and ran.

"Boy, those things left there, every one of 'em at the same time," he related. "We went down off that hill just as fast as we could ride. Didn't want to go that fast, 'cause it was a rocky hill. Not far from the bottom—three-quarters of a mile, I imagine—we got 'em circled. It was pretty exciting for a minute or two."

With the Southwest so arid and watering places so far apart, dry drives were not uncommon. Maybe no twentieth-century drover ever faced a seventy-nine-mile stretch of hell, as did cowboys on the old Goodnight-Loving Trail, but the region still had plenty of searing alkali to curse. When night fell and the thirsty cattle bawled and milled instead of resting, a stampede could erupt at any moment, especially if the wind shifted and the animals caught whiff of a water hole.

Buck Murrah of West Pyle Cattle Company knew just what kind of trouble a thirsty herd could be. Receiving 3,700 steers in the parched salt flats north of Van Horn on a bitterly cold day in 1934, Murrah and his fellow hands were glad the delivering cowboys decided to stick around for the night. After all, these beeves were wild *corrientes* fresh out of Mexico, every one of them dry for water and ready to run, and the Murrah outfit would face a challenge of its own come daybreak. With such an unruly herd, it would be a tough day's drive on to the West Pyle country and pasturage.

As dark fell and the chill factor plummeted, Murrah bundled up against the biting wind and rode out from camp to stand guard.

"That was an enormous bunch of cattle to handle in one herd," he remembered. "They hadn't had any water in two or three days and they'd crossed the river [Rio Grande] and come a long ways."

Abruptly, they were gone, thousands of beeves swallowed by the night.

"You take 3,700 steers running and, by God, you can almost still hear that rumble," said Murrah. "That many cattle, that many feet hitting the ground, sounds worse than any thunderstorm you ever heard. They hit a barbed wire fence and just cleaned it out for two or three miles. They got to running right down it and you couldn't even see a fence there the next morning."

Bob Cage, boss of the other outfit, immediately found Murrah in the swirling dust. "Buck, you think you can find and get them cattle back in this pasture by dark?" he asked.

"Just all depends on how far they run," said Murrah.

Summoning several cowboys, Murrah wheeled his horse and led the chase back down the trail toward Mexico. Miles away, they caught up with half the herd and brought it under control. Throwing the beeves into a basin sheltered from the wind, Murrah and a few hands pressed on.

"I had to ride a horse in a lope fifteen miles before we caught the leaders," he recalled. "They run fifteen miles *that night.* I trailed on ahead of them across a flat, looking for tracks still going back [to Mexico]. I saw that there wasn't any, so we knew then we had 'em all."

Despite the harried, sleepless night, Murrah and the drovers had no choice but to point the beeves back to the north at first light. A brutal day later, they finally reached camp.

A herd, thirsty or not, was especially sensitive to varmints and unfriendly insects. Maybe a fox would sprint by in the night or a skunk or jackrabbit would jump out of a bush; maybe heel flies would descend or a swarm of bees would attack. For cowboys watching over an anxious herd, the result was often the same. "*Anything* can spook 'em," lamented Seth Young, a drover from age fourteen.

When Bud Mayes pointed several hundred steers through the scrub brush of Live Oak Creek in Crockett County one hot day in the 1920s, he never gave a moment's thought to what the beeves might encounter. Nevertheless, disaster was only the poke of a horn away.

"Those things run into a wasp nest and stompeded 'em," said Mayes, who remembered less the excitement of the chase than a more primal matter—self-preservation. "We had a terrible time getting rid of the wasps, but we finally did."

Dogs, big and small, were not a welcome sight along the trail, for few animals could booger a herd quicker. Walter Hoelscher, only a boy of seven on a 1,700-acre spread near Olfen in 1912, saw the trouble two dogs could make for five cowboys passing by with 300 to 400 mixed cattle.

"Those dogs was laying there and they jumped in that herd," he remembered. "Cattle just went everywhere."

Walter Hoelscher in 1990.

Such incidents prompted some outfits to scout ahead when a herd neared a house or community. Still, even forethought wasn't always enough to circumvent disaster, as drover Jim Stroup found out after riding into Lockney in advance of a herd on a long-ago drive.

"I run up to this house and there was some kiddos there and they had a little ol' white dog, a spitz," he related. "I tried to explain to that woman that we was bringing these cattle by and they was easily scared. I told her, 'Be *sure* and keep that dog inside.'"

Returning to the herd, Stroup helped point the animals on toward the house, only to face an outburst.

"We'd just got about even with the yard, and those kids was just gathered up around the door looking," he remembered. "I guess they took the hook off and let the dog out, and out he came."

It took the cowhands more than two days to round up the animals scattered in the inevitable stampede.

Trouble often brewed when a herd entered a community, for people and high-strung beeves were seldom a good mix. To a certain degree, drovers might keep a tight rein on the herd, but they couldn't control the local residents.

Passing through Ingram with 800 head about 1923, Alton Davis and a dozen other hands carefully guarded the herd's flanks. Still, it wasn't enough to stave off adversity.

"There was a lot of people sitting out on their porch or standing out in the yard looking at them cattle," Davis recalled. "Well, somebody come out and slammed the door. Them cattle just turned and went right back the other way. I mean, we had cattle all over that place."

When beeves stampeded in town, it wasn't a pretty sight. Bill Davidson, astride a little Texas horse, could only watch helplessly as 3,000 to 4,000 big steers ran wild one day in a small Oklahoma city.

"All them clothes lines was hanging out full and, hell, they run over 'em," he recalled. "I couldn't even rope one; my horse wasn't big enough to handle 'em."

When a horde of crazed steers stormed away with clothes streaming from every horn, a cowboy was in for an earful from townspeople.

"There was a lot of women in little ol' Spofford, and they'd hang their clothes out on the line," recalled Leonard Hernandez, who frequently drove herds down the fenced railroad right-of-way through town. "Them steers would be tired and mad. They'd jump over the fence and tear up all them ol' clothes lines. Them women would get mad. Oh boy, they'd cuss us."

Imprudent people, whether in a city or along a country road, were always a threat to incite a stampede. About 1939, Frank Derrick and another drover were crossing 200 steers over a dry stretch of the Big Red in the Panhandle when a motorist accelerated a truck across a rattling bridge at their flank. The beeves immediately fled.

Willard Renfro fared little better in the early 1920s as he and Alvin Neal held 210 cows and steers overnight in a country lane near Menard.

"That night someone come through there in an old Model T," said Renfro. "You could hear it a mile before it got to you. I guess those ol' boys had been drinking. They was blowing the horn and hollering. Durn, the cattle scattered all over that country. After the dust cleared off, you could see 'em going across those fields and farmyards."

It took the drovers hours to track down the last of the terrified animals.

Orval Sparks, pursuing runaways into a cotton field in Concho County about 1928, was less worried about his tally book than he was the load of buckshot staring him in the face. As he and another drover had urged the herd down a country road, a Model T had rumbled by and a barking dog in back had launched the 150 steers into flight. Now, as the beeves trampled the cotton, a farmer brandished a shotgun.

"Get out of there or I'm gonna kill you!" the man threatened.

"I'm doing my best!" pleaded Sparks, who, even as he stayed on the wrong end of the barrel, understood the farmer's anger.

"He was holding his shotgun, and I was just a-workin' like hell trying to get 'em out," Sparks recalled. "I don't blame him for being mad, but I couldn't help it."

Sometimes cattle needed no help in finding a reason to bolt, for they were adept at spooking themselves. Perhaps their hooves would clomp against a bridge, or a single cow would find a suddenly popping limb. All too often, it was the only excuse a restless herd needed, as Charlie Drennan and a dozen other cowboys could verify after a 1937 incident at the railroad stockyards near Lamesa.

Jeff Dowell and Charlie Drennan on the Merchant Ranch in Reagan County in 1936. (courtesy, Mrs. Charlie Drennan)

Unloading 2,800 long-horned Mexican *corrientes* from a train, the drovers split the beeves into two herds and started them out the gate for a rainy day's drive.

"I never had seen that many steers in a bunch," recalled Drennan, who was riding point. "And oooh, they was crazy and wild. [In the pasture] they'd start running when you'd get within half a mile of 'em."

As the beeves marched across a thirty-acre trap littered with tin cans, they quickly displayed their skittish nature.

"Them ol' steers began to hit them cans, and man alive, them ol' steers run, their tongues hanging out," remembered Drennan. "It was nearly deafening."

As his horse jumped and ran with the leaders, Drennan seized his rope and slapped it on his chaps.

"I was riding a great big horse called Dutch," he recalled. "He weighed 1,200, I guess. He was sure a good horse, but he was afraid of them steers. I was gonna hold the lead, but I couldn't. I tried to stay with the front ones and whip 'em back, slow 'em up to where the bunch could catch up. But we was plum' out to the A-Bar headquarters five miles out of town by the time we quietened 'em down."

Although cattle were prone to run even on a clear, moonlit night, cowboys feared most the onslaught of severe weather, which triggered more stampedes along more trails than any other factor. "Between the rumbling, roaring, and rattling of hoofs, horns, thunder, and lightning, it made an old cow-puncher long for headquarters or to be in his line camp," lamented nineteenth-century drover S. H. Woods in *The Trail Drivers of Texas.*

Bud Mayes, cowboying a generation later, understood Woods' misery. Headed down the Pecos River for Sheffield with 600 to 700 cows and calves, Mayes and his outfit bunched the herd as dark fell one evening.

"About the time we got 'em settled down for the night, it come the durndest rain you ever saw," remembered Mayes. "Two ol' boys was standing guard and we got up and went out there and tried to help do something with 'em. It started lightning and thundering and the cattle just scattered and went up a canyon. It was so dark that you couldn't even see where you was a-goin', except whenever that lightning would hit, so we just let 'em go and went back to the chuck wagon. The cook had a fire built, but it'd rained so hard it washed the fire out."

By the early 1930s when railroads crisscrossed the region, trains had become almost as notorious as thunderstorms for their fiendish effects on herds. The sheer size of this barreling wall, the roar of its frantically grinding wheels, the piercing screech of a loose rail sagging to the passing tons, the mournful blare of a sudden whistle—one and all, they were invitations to whirl and dance a devil's waltz all the way to the horizon.

"We had an engineer blow a whistle one time, and our cattle took off like a ruptured duck," recalled Pecos River cowboy Jim Witt, who drove herds to the railroad at Pyote in the early 1930s. "They was calves, up to yearlings, 717 head. That damned engineer blew that whistle and they went across that highway. It was a wonder a car didn't hit one of 'em."

With train crews of the era accustomed to freighting cattle, some drovers believed the injudicious use of a whistle didn't always stem from ignorance. As he held up a herd one day to let a train back up on a side track at Floydada, Jim Stroup was dismayed by what he witnessed.

"I saw that engineer just reach up and get that [whistle] string and pull it," he related. "He did it a-purpose and he let it go a long time. The horses went crazy and the cattle did too. We was a day or two getting all those together and we was fined for not getting our boxcars shipped out."

Ralph Davis, cowboying for the White and Swearington outfit of Howard County in the 1920s, could commiserate with Stroup. Bound for the railroad at Big Spring with 800 calves, Davis and his fellow drovers lightened their work by trailing the mother cows along as well, a common practice to facilitate better cooperation in a young herd.

Ralph Davis on the U Ranch in the late 1920s. (courtesy, Ralph Davis)

Reaching the stock pens and shipping the calves, the drovers pointed the cows back down the "cattle drive," a 200-foot-wide trail through town.

"Just as we got about half of 'em across the railroad tracks, the train come along and split 'em up," narrated Davis. "He blew his whistle just as loud as he could toot it; I guess he had a big kick out of it. Anyway, the cows headed south. I was on the front end, and we run with them ol' cows and tried to hold 'em up, but you couldn't. They went up there and just went around and around in a woman's yard and tore down a clothesline. She had all her clothes hanging on it."

Despite the mill, Davis' troubles were far from over.

"One ol' cow went down in what they call Jones Valley and got with somebody's milk cow that they had staked," he related. "[Another cowhand] sent me after her, and by the time I got there she was plenty on the peck. She'd just run me off."

Before long, the second cowboy came riding up in a lope. "Are you scared of her?" he chided.

"Naw, not as long as I can stay away from her."

With an impatient sigh, the other hand reined his mount for the runaway.

"He was riding a little ol' horse they called Red Hoy, a chunky thing that couldn't run fast," remembered Davis. "He rode up there and whipped his chaps leg with his rope and that ol' cow come a-runnin'. He was gonna hold his own but seen he couldn't. He turned and took off and that cow caught up with that horse. She ripped that ol' horse across the rump and just lifted him up from behind with her horns. I know she took him a hundred or two hundred feet with his hind feet raised off the ground—he was just a-runnin' in front."

When it was all over, not only did the cowboy have an injured horse and a red face, but he had to swallow his pride and turn to Davis. "Look," he said sheepishly, "just leave that ol' sister there."

Even so, the train-spooked animal continued to prowl the milk pen and stir up trouble. "The sheriff had to go down there and kill that cow that night before the guy could get his milk cow," recalled Davis.

Near Barnhart in 1932, an ill-advised train whistle also generated desperate moments for Louis Baker. Riding point as he approached a railroad bend with 1,120 cows, he whirled at a sudden commotion up-track.

"Look out!" he cried. "Yonder comes a train!"

His warning came too late. "I run in front of 'em and cut 'em back so the train wouldn't split 'em," he recounted, "and when I did, that train got there and [the engineer] reached up and blowed that horn. And all them cattle broke to run."

Now, there was only one thing to do—overtake the leaders before they plowed into a trap fence dead ahead. Recalled Baker:

> Boy, we had to get to the front of 'em. We run up to this durn ditch about two or three feet deep and Herman Derrick couldn't get his horse to jump off there. I just run up and hit his horse and knocked him off in it and then I come in behind him. Then I beat him to this-here gap [in the trap fence],

reached down with my rope, and caught [the drop-gap gate] and jerked it up. These calves began to hit it and there I was, tied up right out in the middle of 'em. Boy, they piled in there, but we got 'em all settled in about an hour's time.

Even if an engineer refrained from foolishly blowing a horn, a hurtling train could deal a tired drover a lot of misery.

"We was trying to cross the Canadian River a mile or two south of Logan [New Mexico] with a bunch of cattle in '28," remembered Bill Shields. "The river was up and they wouldn't allow but eight or ten cows on this bridge at a time. We had men out in the center to hold 'em up, just get eight on at a time. A train come along and scared 'em. They tore a fence down all the way back to Logan and scattered all over the country."

When a locomotive suddenly exploded out of the night onto an unsuspecting herd, a drover faced not only inconvenience but real peril. Sometimes an inexperienced hand on a good horse was better than a top hand on a lesser animal, as fifteen-year-old Seth Young of the McBee outfit proved in a 1917 incident in Kinney County.

"I was riding the point that night on a big sorrel horse, about 1,100 pounds," recounted Young, one of several drovers with the herd. "Oh, he was a good cow horse, fast. There wasn't a damned one of 'em had a horse like I was riding, I guarantee. The leaders had just run under a [railroad] bridge to get a little water and a train came along. It was there before you knew it. They'd never seen a train or heard one, and that scared 'em and they all turned back just like one cow."

In the dust and bedlam that followed, the fledgling cowhand found himself lost in the dark amid hundreds of charging animals.

"I'd had the left point," he recalled, "and in about five minutes I was riding the right point—they turned back through themselves."

Nevertheless, Young's superior horse kept its balance and quickly responded when he pushed hard for the leaders. "I circled those cows to the left," he remembered, "and we kept 'em running in a circle and in a little bit they settled down. Next morning, [owner] Uncle Will McBee told me, 'Good thing you was riding that sorrel.'"

Any cowboy was only as good as his horse, and whenever he was caught in a mass of demon-blooded runaways bumping him left and right, his chances of seeing another sunrise were no better than the strength and poise of his mount. Twelve-year-old Lewis Doran, trapped in a seething herd fleeing a train in Eden in the late 1910s, fortunately was astride a stout animal.

There was no hint as he held position in a fenced lane on the approach to the stockyards that the 500 big longhorns would bolt. Suddenly a train appeared, belching steam and thundering over cross ties, and the cows whirled and ran before he knew what was happening.

"I was right in the middle of 'em," remembered Doran. "Boy, I was scared to death; don't think I wasn't. I just stayed on that ol' horse—I had to. Them wild cattle hit that horse and everything, trying to get over that fence. It's a wonder it hadn't knocked him down, but it didn't. That train had upset that ol' horse and he was scared to death himself. Those cattle laid that fence down and it taken us about four hours to ever get 'em back up there."

Olan George, paralleling the Orient of Texas track southwest of Girvin with 200 heifers about 1926, wasn't so lucky. Caught in a caldron of stampeding brutes unnerved by an oncoming locomotive and its untimely whistle, he went down hard in "the darndest wreck" and stayed down.

"There were just two of us, me and a Mexican boy," he recounted. "I give him credit for being a little smarter than I was, because he got out of the way and I didn't. A cow running from the noise of that train tried to go under that horse, and he slipped and we *all* went down. He had his legs up on the side of that cow and he was on my leg. *I* couldn't get up, *he* couldn't get up, and the *cow* couldn't get up."

By the time the Mexican hand weaved his way through the boiling herd, George was in even more trouble.

"The cow was floundering and the horse was floundering and every time he'd move he'd mash my leg a little bit more. [The other cowboy] finally wanted to know what he could do, and I told him to put his rope on that cow's back legs and drag her out from under that horse. When he did, we all come up together."

The 1930s and early 1940s was a transition period for cowboying; the old ways weren't forgotten yet, but the horse's exclusive role in a cowboy's life was weakening before the encroachment of pickups and cattle trucks. In a few decades, the success of a roundup sometimes would depend as much on a helicopter as it would a horseman.

With mechanization, though, came troubles of which no drover of the Goodnight-Loving Trail could possibly have dreamed.

In the early 1930s, Ralph Davis bossed the roundup of 750 yearlings on the U Ranch in Sterling County with the intent of driving the animals to the railroad.

"We'd eased 'em up there where we wanted to hold 'em in the pasture and just stopped," recounted Davis. "I took them ol' boys aside and I said, 'Now, let's all keep quiet and don't stir these cattle up.'"

Twisting around in the saddle at a sudden, uncomfortable buzz, he lifted his gaze high over the nearby brush and caught the glint of sunlight from an airplane piloted by "Little George" McEntire, son of the U Ranch owner. Little George, although raised on the ranch, had never been able to appreciate the finer aspects of cowboying, preferring the purr of an engine to the moo of a cow. Once, when his father, George McEntire Sr., had asked what it would take to get him on a horse, Little George had replied, "Put wheels on it."

Now, as Little George's craft veered and cut a trail across the sky straight for the skittish yearlings, Davis could only brace himself. Recounted Davis:

"Ol' George come in in his ol' airplane and just went right down about twenty feet over the top of 'em. ['I wasn't quite *that* high,' recalled Little George.] That crazy sucker give 'em a big buzz and it wasn't no holding 'em. Them cattle went west. We tried to hold 'em up for two miles, but it was so brushy you couldn't circle 'em. So we just quit."

If the drovers had looked up from the onrushing herd long enough to consider the newfangled contraption dominating the sky, they might have realized that the sun was fast fading for an Old West already besieged by barbed wire.

Splintering Fences and Midnight Danger

As Green Mankin prepared to ride out to guard 500 cows in a pasture corner between Sonora and Brackettville one long-ago night, he posed a question to his boss, Bug Dunbar.

"If they wanna run, what do you do, Bug?"

"Just sing to 'em," Dunbar replied. "Ride around 'em and sing to 'em."

Green Mankin in 1989.

Later, as the tiring Mankin dismounted near the cattle and rolled a cigarette, the likelihood of a stampede seemed farfetched. After all, not only were the animals gentle, but they had been driven hard and seemed content to chew their cuds in the midnight dark. Still, he was careful not to shake the saddle as he swung back up across his horse and continued his slow ride around the herd. Then, without warning, it happened.

"Sounded like one of them wires broke; maybe the old wires was too tight," recalled Mankin. "Anyhow, them cattle was gone like *that*—disappeared—and wire just went in every direction. We was in a rough, rocky, brushy country and we had thirty-five or thirty-seven we never did find. Bug asked me, 'Did you sing to those cattle?' I said, 'I was singing, yeah; I was singing when they run.' And he said, 'Well, don't you ever sing anymore.'"

With a downed fence to repair and horses likely cut in a tangle of barbed wire, it was a disastrous state of affairs. Still, exhausted drovers often welcomed the sight of a fence, for in its corner they might hold a herd overnight with a minimum of guards. As with Mankin, though, many cowhands found in the location insidious pitfalls that gave them reason to cuss a barbed wire world.

In a corner southwest of Midland one night in 1930, a big herd didn't hear the off-key croon of a drover, but the rumble of thunder—a sound not exactly soothing to a restless mix of bulls, steers, cows, and calves. It was only 10 P.M., but already it was pitch black, and the pouring rain made for a miserable stint in the saddle for hands standing guard at this intersection of three   Scharbauer Ranch pastures. Suddenly, in the twitch of an eye, every animal was on its feet and whirling.

"They started a-runnin'," remembered Slim Vines. "Boy, they tore down those three fences. You could hear those wires popping and the posts breaking off. Everybody got up and got their horse and went out to help hold the herd. But it was dark as it could be and there wasn't no way of telling what you were running into. Some of the boys got in this barbed wire. Horses go crazy when they get tangled in barbed wire—they go to kicking and trying to get away from it, and if it gets wrapped around their feet, it'll ruin 'em."

Unable to give proper chase, the cowboys had to work all three pastures the next day, rounding up and sorting the confusing aggregate of herd stock and native beeves. The experience taught the trail boss an important lesson.

"That old man said, 'Well, I'll tell you one thing about this trail driving I've learned—we're not gonna camp by a fence any more,'" related Vines, one of several disgruntled cowhands with the outfit. "Well, we could have told him that. You don't want to be around a fence when cattle are running."

Nevertheless, after a hard day's drive it was mighty tempting to turn a herd into a convenient corral or a "run-around" for the night. More confining than a pasture corner, a pen could lull weary drovers into believing it was also more secure. Such was not always the case.

Helping two other drovers pen 200 cattle south of San Angelo one night about 1899, Leonard Proctor looked forward to a good night's sleep. After all, he was only seven or so, and he had been doing a man's work alongside his father ever since they had first pointed the animals down-trail. But when a bad storm blew in during the night, sleep became the last of his worries.

"It was thundering and lightning and raining, and the cattle broke out," he remembered. "My daddy and this other fellow got the horses for us. I got a-hold of a bunch of [the runaways], thirty or forty head, I guess, and got 'em held up. I was in a strange country and a little ol' tot, and a stormy night, but I rode 'em and kept 'em together until morning. Of course, they did the same thing, but it was a couple of days before we got the cattle together again."

Thomas Henderson, at six too young to make much of a hand, nevertheless gained his own lasting memory of a corral stampede sixteen miles south of Marathon in 1914.

"It'd been raining and nobody had slept in a week, and Papa thought those guys might get a little rest if they put those cattle in this big holding pen," he recalled. "Everybody was wet and their beds was so wet they couldn't sleep in 'em. They hopped under the wagon and drank coffee and smoked cigarettes and cussed because they was cold and wet. It started raining again and a big clap of thunder caused those damned animals to run. They hit that fence full force and trampled it over. They got away and it crippled a bunch of 'em."

Green Mankin and a drover named Blackie, holding seventy-five or eighty cows in a cedar-pole corral in the Ozona country one night in the 1920s, had a ringside seat for a breakout. Remembered Mankin:

> They'd been cut off from their calves two days before, and they was a-bawlin' and circling the pen all the time. It was cold, so we had taken our

bedrolls and we pulled 'em up on the south side right against the fence. It was a lot warmer that way. Along about midnight, them ol' cows got to running. They'd hit that fence and it'd pop and crack. It was getting worse, and Blackie sat up and he was awfully excited. "They're gonna go, Green, they're gonna go!"

I said, "Hell, I can't help it; I can't do anything about it." I was cold and I didn't want to be up.

The moon was shining just as bright, but the wind was blowing like the dickens. Directly—damn them cattle—they hit that fence and the cedar posts just went ever' direction. I raised up right quick and I saw Blackie. He had on long-handled underwear and his shirt and he was following the cattle. He was leaving out, and had a boot in each hand and his shirttail was just flying.

Them cattle was done gone. Wasn't any use of me doing *anything*. I just laid back down.

When confined cattle leveled a fence, they often cut a swath of destruction through the night. As the sun sank over Cleo in Kimble County one spring, several cowhands received a herd and secured the bony animals in the railroad stock pens. When an electrical storm struck in the night, the cattle broke free and stampeded toward a nearby school and cemetery.

"They took that schoolyard fence and just laid it over," recalled Willard Renfro, who mounted up and set out in pursuit. "We tried to just hold 'em up around that schoolyard, but they went on in the cemetery. We went out there the next morning and some of those markers was turned over. We straightened 'em up the best we could and fixed the schoolyard fence. The worse thing was the privy—it looked like they *all* took a lick at it. The doors was even knocked off."

Sometimes cattle paid a heavy price for bursting free of a corral, as seventeen-year-old Marvin Hooper discovered in 1918 after helping pen 3,000 cows north of Lovington, New Mexico, on a drive across the Staked Plains.

"Along in the night," he recalled, "there come an electric storm, a bad one. Those cattle got to milling and about two or three o'clock in the morning, they broke out of that pen and just went to running everywhere. Three of 'em got killed; the others run over 'em."

Like a stumbling cow, a sleeping cowboy could find his life hanging in the balance at such a time, for his bedding might lie in the very path of the onrushing crush of hooves. Awakened suddenly, addled and disoriented, he might have only seconds to run for cover—the very situation Seth Young once faced twelve miles south of Rocksprings. Fortunately, the young cowhand was in the company of his uncle, a seasoned hand who knew how to gather his wits quickly.

Turning their drove of 100 cows into a half-acre runaround with a high pole fence, the two drovers stretched out nearby in a discarded wagon bed that rested on the ground. Well into the night, the older man awoke to the groaning of poles and quickly roused Young.

"Let's get up!" he cried.

As the fence splintered and began to give way, the drovers fled into the dark.

"He got me behind a big oak tree," recalled Young, "so if they come out over the fence by us, they couldn't knock us down. But they went out on the north side, and we was on the east side. They was about fifty yards from us when they broke out and run across a bermuda grass [patch]."

Sometimes a herd breached a corral fence and bore straight for the chuck wagon, a development a cowhand was not soon to forget. As the sun sank during a drive from Mason to Brady in 1919, sixteen-year-old Si Loeffler helped corral 300 heifers and steer calves in adjacent pens. One was a water lot, the other a corral with a six-foot fence of rock. As the drovers prepared their bedrolls around the chuck wagon, the trail boss turned to the youthful Loeffler.

"Si," he said, "I'm gonna unroll my bedroll right by the side of yours. I hope these calves don't stompede, but if they do, why, I know you'll wake up before I will and you can kick me and wake me up so we won't get run over."

Sure enough, two hours past midnight Loeffler stirred to "the durndest rumbling" he had ever heard.

"Those calves in that rock pen just laid that rock pen flat," he recalled. "When they stompeded, the others [in the water lot] did too and the horses went with 'em. We got under the chuck wagon. They ran all around us, and some of 'em bumped the wagon and stomped our beds."

In any stampede, whether from a corral or a corner or open bed grounds, a cowboy afoot could be in dire straits. "It don't make a dang what's in front of them cattle; they won't turn," noted one old cowhand.

As Clarence Arrott helped hold a herd south of Marathon one night about 1916, a guard anxious for a smoke unwisely struck a match near the resting animals. "The cattle broke and run and come over and went all the way around the chuck box," recalled Arrott. "The ol' boys that was in the bed had to take high country."

It was not an isolated occurrence. On a drive in the San Saba River country about 1921, Loeffler watched elderly cowman Charlie Kothmann stretch out for the night in the safest spot he could find—under the chuck wagon. Loeffler, by now in his late teens and a top hand, tossed his own bedroll down under the open sky and fell asleep. Sometime after midnight, the roar of 200 running steers shook every man in camp out of bed.

"The herd broke in two and one part of 'em came our way," remembered Loeffler. "And that old man—he was close to eighty—got up and I can still see him by the light of that campfire. He had long gray hair and a full beard, and he was trying to climb a tree to get out of those steers' way."

Fortunately, the cowboys got the raging herd under control in time. Still, a tree was a handy thing to have around when such an unyielding force came charging, as Alton Davis could testify.

In the early 1920s Davis and a dozen other YO drovers, bound for Kerrville with 800 big steers, turned their herd into a 1,000-acre trap in the forested Hill Country near Ingram. Guarding against stampede, the boss dispatched hands to each of the five or six corners. Davis and his partner, reaching their assigned position, took additional precautions even as they readied for a peaceful night.

"We hitched our horses where they could break loose," recalled Davis.

As dark fell, the two men drifted off into weary oblivion, only to sit up wide-eyed at a loud rumbling long before daylight. Whirling to the shadows, they recognized the tumult as an army of unrelenting hooves drawing near.

"Hell, them cattle was just like a cyclone a-comin'," Davis remembered.

In desperation, the cowhands clambered into a big live oak, where they looked down through the rising dust as the herd hurtled by. As planned, their horses broke free and escaped, but a drover in the next corner hadn't been so prudent.

"He tied his horse solid," recalled Davis. "Them cattle run over that horse and just cut him all to pieces with their hooves, just ruined him."

Alton Davis in 1990.

Even to a mounted cowboy, a barreling horde of oncoming beeves could be daunting. Faced with being swept up in the maelstrom, a wise hand might cast aside his horse, along with any foolish notions of valor, and seek the nearest shelter. Even so, he might escape the crushing swarm by only the narrowest of margins.

Si Loeffler, on his baptismal drive in 1919, found himself riding guard over 258 big steers one night in a 400-acre trap in Mason County. Another drover brought his horse abreast of Loeffler's, and the two of them paused in the shadows to talk a spell.

"It was a bright, moonlight night, and we were just sitting there on our horses, blowing," related Loeffler. "All of a sudden, those dat-gum steers started stompeding. And they came right our way."

S. M. "Si" Loeffler about 1920. (courtesy, Nancy Loeffler)

Realizing the danger of trying to outrun the herd, the drovers quickly scanned the terrain and found a bouldered ledge nearby. Falling away less than a yard, it stretched eight feet across the very path of the charging steers. Whirling to the nearing leaders, Loeffler, like his partner, made a choice—he sprang from his horse, gave the reins a quick wrap around the animal's neck, and dived for the ledge's base. Flattening himself, he lay there feeling the quake of a thousand hooves and waited for the deadly onslaught.

"We just laid right against those rocks as close as we could," Loeffler recalled, "and you could still see those steers jumping over those rocks above us. Luckily, the horses just ran off about a hundred yards and got out of the steers' way."

When the earth tremor finally died away, the two hands stood up in the settling dust and found one another shaken but uninjured.

A drover, in trying to cope with a runaway herd, sometimes flew out of the saddle for all the wrong reasons. "There'd be fellows whose horse stepped in a hole," explained Otis Coggins. "After a stompede, you'd have two or three men afoot with horses gone."

Every drover accepted danger as part of the job, but it was still mighty troubling to see a man's horse come trotting in alone after a night stampede, especially one brought on by thunder and lightning. Even if the rider had survived the fall, he was afoot in a storm in hostile backcountry that likely was too dark to navigate. Not only was he subject to shock stemming from possible injuries, he was a prime candidate for hypothermia.

Coggins once found himself in just such a predicament. Riding guard through the mud near Eagle Pass one night about 1932, he pulled his hat low over his brow against a brutal storm. He could read trouble in the herd; all 800 cows were on edge, punished by the same rain and hail that beat rhythmically on his shoulders. Even more ominous, thunder was blaring, and from the boiling clouds came wicked jags of lightning.

Suddenly, they were off, tearing through the night, 3,200 hooves dispersing clods of mud on a breakneck pace "to hell and gone."

Hanging on as his horse jumped and ran with the cattle, Coggins took control of the animal and rode hard for the leaders through scrub brush and yucca. A harried mile later, his horse stepped in a hole and suddenly they were down, a squealing horse and a numbed rider. Before Coggins could seize the dragging reins, the gelding was on its feet and gone, leaving him stranded in a dark desert racked by storm.

Shaken but unhurt, he stood and scanned the countryside through the pouring rain; in any cow camp, the cook was responsible for keeping a lighted lantern sitting on the chuck box or hanging from the wagon bows. But on this unfriendly night, Coggins saw nothing but shadowy yucca standing against a black veil.

Even though camp was only a twenty-minute walk away, he needed the light of day to get his bearings. The trouble was, it was only 3 A.M., and in a storm of this magnitude, it was a devil of a long time till daybreak. Sooner or later, the other riders would come in search, but with a herd of crazed cows on their hands, it might be hours before they missed him.

There was only one thing to do.

"I crawled up under an ol' dagger [yucca]," Coggins recalled. "It was a-rainin' and a-thunderin' and lightning. I stayed till daylight. Just as I could see light, I got my direction and walked into camp. They was looking for me; they'd got the herd settled down, but I think we lost about thirty head. When the horse wrangler come in with the horses, he brought my horse in with him."

Sometimes a dislodged rider went down in the face of hundreds of flailing hooves—a desperate situation that few drovers ever lived to tell about. Alphonzo Dunnahoo, a cowboy from the age of thirteen in 1914, was one of the lucky ones.

Shutting the gate on 200 head of cattle on the Wimberley Ranch twelve miles south of Loraine about 1929, Dunnahoo paused in the saddle to study them across the pole fence. They were wild and ornery, a bunch of outlaw cows from the Bell Ranch in New Mexico, but in a few days they would be inside a jostling railroad car headed for the horizon.

Suddenly the unpredictable animals exploded through the fence and barreled into his horse. As he fell from the saddle, a crashing pole caught Dunnahoo flush in the head and the world went dark. "Knocked me cold," he recalled six decades later. "I've still got a scar on my head."

It was a small price to pay in exchange for his life; only the protection of a standing section of fence kept him from being crushed by the hooves.

The force generated by a stampeding herd was tremendous, but a horse suddenly impacting the ground at the speed of an all-out gallop could be just as treacherous for its rider. All too often, a cowboy dragged himself up only to wince from the pain of a torn ligament or broken bone.

Fred McClellan and Earnest Clifton, helping three other hands hold a herd on the Spade Ranch near Colorado City about 1934, had no reason to suspect that within minutes one of them would be crippled for a while. After all, it was midday, most of the 2,000 yearlings were lying down, and the sky held no hint of threat. Nevertheless, the animals suddenly sprang to their feet and bolted. Pursuing, McClellan lost sight of Clifton in the frenzy and dust, but after the herd took up a mill, a couple of drovers backtracked and found the missing hand.

"His horse stepped in a hole and fell," remembered McClellan. "It broke his leg, and they just bundled him up."

Otis Coggins knew well the pain of a sudden horse fall in the chase for the leaders; he also knew his relative good fortune in merely surviving a late-1920s stampede so insidious that thirty cattle carcasses were left to mark the runaways' South Texas trail.

"We was on night guard and holding 'em pretty close to a ranch house," he recalled. I think an ol' rooster flapped his wings and crowed. That's what set them off."

A thousand strong, the steers forged through the night, the stronger crushing the weaker in a mad race down a railroad track. Suddenly there was only a narrow trestle ahead, and left and right, dozens of beeves plummeted into the dark.

"They broke their backs, and broke legs, and some of 'em got their horns knocked off," recalled Coggins.

Otis Coggins in 1990.

Clinging stubbornly to the side of the surging herd, Coggins took his galloping horse down the bank of the unexpected arroyo and out again, only to feel his saddle abruptly drop out from under him. He hit the turf viciously, breaking his collarbone. Still, there was a herd to save, and his horse had regained its feet to hold its ground just yards away. Mounting up, Coggins resumed the chase and helped circle the steers in a big open field.

On an extended drive, especially through a remote area where medical help wasn't available, a bunged-up cowboy (even one without life-threatening injuries) was a considerable burden. Often, there was no recourse but to lay him in the chuck wagon for a jolting ride down-trail while the shorthanded drovers brought up the beeves. Such a misfortune befell an outfit that included Coggins as it pushed north through Coahuila, Mexico, in 1934.

A week's drive south of Piedras Negras and the Texas border, Coggins and two dozen other drovers bunched the beeves for the night. There were 1,800 head, unruly steers of longhorn-brahman mix, and if they boogered in this unfenced country, they might not slow till they splashed into the Rio Grande, eighty miles distant.

Coggins, asleep in camp, never heard the lone steer belch in the night, but the sudden noise was enough to send every animal fleeing.

Riding out to help, he quickly overtook the drags and began to creep up along the herd's flank. As the chase lingered, the swirling dark and thick dust blinded him to the stumbling of his partners' horses. Several riders went down, a couple catching passing hooves as they wallowed in the dirt. By the time Coggins helped circle the cattle five miles from camp, the toll for keeping the herd intact was sprawled back up-trail—thirty dead or crippled beeves and several bruised cowboys, three or four with broken limbs that would buy the men a rough ride in the chuck wagon for a few days.

If any of the injured hands had a typical cowboy's outlook, he probably managed a painful grin. After all, one of these days over a plate of beans, he could tell how his misfortune had all begun with the gastrointestinal workings of a single gassy steer.

Greenhorns, Pranks, and Pitching Horses

Reaching Three Wells southeast of Midland in advance of a Quien Sabe herd sometime before 1906, a chuck wagon creaked to a halt near a trio of windmills that had given the site its name. The driver, a cook new to the outfit, unhitched the team, draped the harnesses over the front wheel, and set up camp. As he stooped over his cook fire, he looked up to find the drovers turning their 400 beeves into the water lot for the night.

Later, as the hands downed a hearty meal around the chuck wagon, they whispered and nodded. They couldn't complain about the food, but they could spot a greenhorn a mile away—and the cook was as green as they came. Even after supper, the drovers watched and listened, and when the jittery fellow eyed the corral nervously, muttered something about a stampede, and set off with his bedroll in search of a safe sleeping place, they couldn't keep from snickering. When he finally returned to the wagon and crawled underneath, the stage was set for mischief.

Dark fell, and as the cook drifted off to fitful sleep, a couple of cowboys eased out of their beds and crept to the wagon. They had hatched a plan sure to bring roars of laughter—they would fool the sleeping cook into thinking a stampede was at hand.

"They got this harness and just went to shaking it and wiggling the wagon tongue," said Billy Rankin, whose father was along on the drive. "They was hollering 'Whoa! Whoa!' and them kind of things. They made so much racket—and the cook too in bumping his head on the wagon and running and all—that the cattle *did* run off."

Despite unexpected consequences, pranks were common on the range and trail, for a cowboy usually had a funny bone as broad as the backside of an ornery old bull. He might pay a dear price sometimes—a whole night chasing stampeding cattle maybe, or a day or two dodging retaliation or a chewing-out from the boss—but he usually persisted in creating humor.

"There was always some kind of a prankster amongst every group," noted cowhand Max Reed.

Like the Quien Sabe cook, greenhorns were always a prime target for pranks, for they were usually young, gullible, and vulnerable. Equally important, they were little threat to mete out retribution, and cowboys considered a little good-natured "hoorawing," or teasing, a rite of passage for a tenderfoot. Certainly, it had been so in their own tender years.

More often than not, a greenhorn unwittingly gave cowboys plenty of ammunition about which to kid him. Ted Powers, later to be a rodeo star, recalled his first night as a sixteen-year-old roundup hand with the T Half Circle in Sutton County in 1923:

They was all sitting around the fire shooting bull, and I was a stranger, of course. It was most all grown men, and I'd never been in that country, and I got to feeling pretty lonesome. I got my bedroll out of the wagon and asked my boss, Gus Love, "Where can I roll my bed?" He stopped and looked at me about a minute before he answered me. He grinned and said, "Son, there's fifty sections in this pasture—you just pick you out a spot." I learned quick not to ask silly questions.

Ted Powers in 1989.

Learning to subdue immature impulses, however, was another matter. When young Powers' horse went lame on a cattle drive, T Half Circle manager Willie Wilkinson cut him out the best gelding in the outfit—Ol' White Man, a snow-white animal that was Wilkinson's own.

"We had that herd going good down a draw, and boy, I felt good sitting on that good grain-fed horse," recounted Powers. "There's a lot of difference from an ol' grass-fed, big-bellied horse, and he looked so pretty. The sun was going down behind us and I could see my shadow off out there. I don't guess there ever was a cowboy while he was young didn't look at his shadow. I was riding along there looking at my shadow; I'd set my hat one way and then another, trying to make it look better."

But while Powers was primping, the cattle were straying.

"Shorty!" Wilkinson hollered to the diminutive Powers. "Shorty! Come back over here and help with these cattle!"

Embarrassed, Powers urged his horse back into proper position, only to hear Wilkinson herald his approach to the whole outfit: "Riding along there like King Solomon on that white horse!"

The result was inevitable. "That tickled those cowboys and they called me King Solomon for about a week," recalled Powers. "I sure was careful about looking at my shadow from then on."

Generally, a dyed-in-the-wool tenderfoot was more liability than asset. "You could take two or three cowboys and work more cattle than you could with a dozen greenhorns out of the city," noted Tyson Midkiff. "You get a bunch of greenhorns out there and they got in your way."

Still, every boss had been a greenhorn himself once, so he was usually patient in developing a young hand. Initially, he might hide the young man's deficiencies by assigning him menial tasks such as milking cows, hauling firewood, or digging postholes—sometimes for no more compensation than room and board. If a tenderfoot showed good knowledge of horses, the boss might let him take part in a roundup or cattle drive as a horse wrangler, an important job in which he alone was responsible for the remuda. If the lad showed real promise and a herd was on the move, it was a good idea to position him on drag, where he could soak up a little experience along with the alkali.

Sometimes, however, a young "cowboy-for-to-be" found himself involved in a chore unbefitting even the lowliest of ranch hands.

"I was always wanting to get me a cowboy job, but from the age of thirteen to about seventeen, I'd just have to do cowboy work on the weekends," said Paul Patterson. "I remember how humiliated I was when I thought I had this riding cowboy job with Alvaro Yates. He was going to put me on [the payroll]—but he had me walk along from Upland [in Upton County] to Stanton and drive a flock of turkeys. There's a lot of humiliation in trying to be a cowboy besides getting thrown off and hurt."

Even in a riding job, a greenhorn had obstacles to overcome. "They'd put him on an ol' horse that you couldn't make a hand on," recalled Ralph Davis.

A lot of cowhands, recalling their own early days with an outfit, sympathized with a kid cast to such a fate.

"Lots of young boys would go to work on a ranch and they'd ask him what kind of hand he was," noted Frank Derrick. "He'd say, 'Well, what kind of horses you gonna furnish me?' You couldn't be a cowboy without a good horse."

Even if a tenderfoot endured the sorry mounts, ignoble chores, and constant hoorawing, he often faced a gauntlet of grinning cowboys ready to administer a rite of initiation.

"They'd make him go between them and they'd get a spat at him with their leggings if he was sure 'nough a greenhorn," recounted Charlie Drennan.

It was all a test of a tenderfoot's mettle, and he soon found out whether or not he was cut out to be a cowboy. Some passed, but others looked for the nearest trail out.

"I've seen a-many a ol' kid roll that bedroll up and go home to mama," said Frank Yeary.

A young hand who toughed it out usually earned the cowboys' respect. Unless he was a know-it-all, the older hands took him under wing and taught him not only the cow business, but right and wrong. They might continue to hooraw him, but it was always in good fun.

"I never did try to degrade a kid," said Shorty Northcutt. "A few of 'em, I've got bucked off, but it wasn't because I hated the kid; I just figured he needed a lesson. There wasn't many of us would put up with a smart aleck; we'd get even with 'em some way or another."

On the Spade Ranch near Colorado City long ago, a greenhorn quickly revealed himself as just the sort who needed to be set straight. Recalled Northcutt:

> He was a smart aleck who thought he could ride pretty good, but he couldn't. He was fixing to leave out from the ranch one morning, and dat-gum, he come out with a new saddle and put it on this ol' horse. He just barely could ride him, you know. His spurs had rowels great big around, them ol'

Mexican spurs. So when he come out the gate, he jobbed 'em in [to the horse] and says, "Oh yes, blankety-blank! Oh yes, blankety-blank!" He was bucking down the road and that ol' horse laid him down. He hit right flat of his back and just knocked the wind out of him. This time all he could do was grunt a little: "*Oh yes, blankety-blank!*"

On another occasion, a young hand exhibited all the characteristics that raised Northcutt's hackles.

"He got on an ol' pony and he just kept tampering with him, acting like he wanted him to pitch," he recounted. "I stood it about as long as I could and I said, 'I'll tell you what—I'll beat you to that cedar tree there.' Man, he just jobbed 'em in him [spurred the horse], and when he did that ol' horse let him down and broke his arm. He just kept asking for it till I figured out some way to let him have it."

Cowboys seldom, if ever, perpetrated a practical joke with malicious intent, but like Northcutt, a lot of them delighted in making another cowhand's horse "break in two," or pitch. Indeed, unless the boss frowned on the practice, it was a prankster's favorite pastime. With the ingenuity of a master inventor, he accomplished the feat in ways obvious and cloaked, from near and afar, but always with a grin and a hooraw.

Often, a bronc didn't need much encouragement to cooperate with the scheme.

"Most of the horses, back those days, you didn't *have* to make 'em pitch—they was gonna pitch a little anyway," recalled Bud Mayes. "I've seen 'em pitch right up to the cook's fire and all of his skillets."

Still, a prankster's method sometimes was as blatant as a swift kick in the rear.

"The ol' boy would be sitting there, not paying no attention," said Otis Coggins, "and you'd slip up behind and kick his horse in the butt. If his horse was bad about pitching, he'd just swallow his head and maybe throw the ol' boy off. And you'd have to catch the horse and come back and the ol' boy would cuss you out good-naturedly, or maybe take after you with the double of his rope."

Usually, though, a fun-seeking cowboy was a little more subtle in his approach. He might toss a thorny tasajillo stalk at a man's horse, or use a stick or other object to gouge a bronc in the flank or in a more sensitive spot— under the tail.

"Certain ol' horses carry their tail up pretty high," noted Thomas Henderson. "You can get a piece of lechuguilla stalk or a sotol stalk two feet long and ride up and stick it under that ol' horse's tail. He'd pitch just like a scalded dog."

The most scheming way of exploiting this Achilles heel of a bronc was the "rimfire," a method known to almost every cowboy in the Southwest.

"Rimfire," said Henderson," works like this: I'll ride up and hand you the end of my rope, and that man we're after is right ahead of us. Then we'll ride up behind him."

"Maybe he'd be riding a kind of skittish horse anyway," said Bob Calcote, who first hired on with a Schleicher County outfit about 1918. "One would be on one side of him and one on the other side, and they'd pull their rope up under the horse's tail."

Nine times out of ten, the bronc responded as planned. "He'd buck and rare [rear] and raise cain, and you'd either have to ride him or get bucked off," said Ralph Davis.

"That ol' boy [astride the bronc] wouldn't know what was happening," said Henderson. "And the boss always asked, 'Who rimfired that horse?' Nobody knew."

Another favorite method of riling a snaky horse was to throw or kick something underfoot. Maybe the threat would be as innocent as a hat, but it usually evoked an on-the-spot rodeo.

"Me and another ol' boy would trade out wrangling on an ol' horse that was a right smart hand to buck anyhow," recalled Jack Pate. "One of us would throw a shovel of ashes under him every morning—kept in pretty good shape that a-way."

"One ol' boy around Odessa," noted Douglas Poage, "would pile up a roll of dirt in the corral gate and then open the gate for you. When you rode out of the corral, he'd kick that dirt under the horse."

New hands Steve Armentrout and Green Mankin, roping out broncs in a corral on the first morning of a 1930s roundup on the 7N's west of Ozona, had no inkling that they would soon face boss Zack Eppler's own brand of gate humor.

"We got in there and boy, my horse was a flea-bitten son-of-a-gun," remembered Armentrout. "We had to tie his foot up to get the saddle on him. But we got him saddled and then we got Green's saddled."

As the roping-out process continued, Armentrout mounted up and tested his bronc. Pleased with how the animal took to a man in the saddle, he confidently awaited the opening of the gate.

Finally, Eppler's voice rang out. "Y'all ready?"

"Yeah," answered a rider.

As the gate screeched open, little did anyone realize that at Eppler's feet was a pile of tow sacks he had soaked in the water trough.

Steve "Slim" Armentrout in 1989.

"Me and Green was the first ones to come out, and he commenced throwing them sacks underfoot," recounted Armentrout. "Oh boy, them horses jumped high as the ceiling. We had this short, heavy-set guy out of Montana [who was] supposed to be a rodeo bronc rider. When them horses come out of there, I think he was about the first one got throwed. Them horses run over him and skinned him up."

As riders went flopping out through the pasture, Armentrout, wearing big-roweled Mexican spurs, tried to gig his heavy Spanish gray under control. Unaccountably, the bronc, with head between its knees, veered straight for the ranch house, situated at the edge of a slope three hundred yards away. Recalled Armentrout:

> I was doing well to ride him. I'm trying to cut that horse in two with them spurs and blood was just pouring down a stream on each side. But I could nearly gut him and he'd just throw his head up yonder a little. He went up to that house, and there was a little ol' porch roof just came down over the open door for a shade. I thought sure that my horse was gonna run in that house. I was fixing to quit him; I done had my right foot out of the stirrup, 'cause that little ol' porch roof wasn't high enough and it would've cut me in two.

Suddenly the most unexpected of things happened.

"A woman come to the door and throwed the dish water out and hit that horse right in the face," remembered Armentrout. "He just stood on his hind feet and whirled and throwed his head up and went back to the pen. He never bucked another jump."

The price for Eppler's prank was not only a few claw marks down the sides of the broncs, but a lot of extra work tracking down the runaways that had spilled their riders.

"Most of 'em had the saddle under their belly," noted Armentrout, "but we found pieces of saddle all over that two-section pasture. We lost about a week gathering them horses and going back to town and getting the saddles fixed up."

Sometimes when a cowboy urged his horse out the gate, he faced not a flying sack or spray of dirt, but a racket loud enough to make any bronc kick to the sky.

"I was riding an ol' bronc one time, and ol' Roy Sheppard tied a tub to the end of his rope and turned me out the gate," recounted Panhandle cowboy Frank Yeary. "He got after me with that old tub and scared that bronc to death. He run me plum' out of the country. I went off the caprock into the breaks, and I never did get that ol' bronc back on top. I had to unsaddle him, turn him loose, and carry my saddle back."

A more devious way of inducing a horse to spill a rider involved tampering with the saddle, a method which allowed the perpetrator to sit back innocently and watch a regular wild west show. Maybe he would secretly slacken the latigo, or strap, that held the all-important cinch in place; with the saddle loose, the victim only had to dig his boot in the stirrup to bring it turning. Not only would the cowboy do a belly flop, but his horse would usually run away, kicking at the strange contraption between its legs.

Another way of sabotaging a cowboy's chances of successfully mounting up and staying astride even a gentle horse was by covertly slipping something under the saddle and blanket. Often it was a cocklebur, sometimes an upside-down horned toad, but the result was the same.

"When that ol' kid got up and got in that saddle and sat down on that thing sticking in that horse," said Joe Lambert, "that horse would down his head and throw him."

126

A hand new to an outfit always had to be on guard until he learned the idiosyncracies of the remuda, for cowboys were notorious for roping out a lively bronc for a new-comer. "Most of them guys that would come in would say, 'I don't want a pitching horse,'" recounted Fish Wilson. "Well, that didn't help you none—they'd just cut 'em to you like they did everybody else." Indeed, the practice of wel-coming a new hand with a mean horse was so common that Fin Cox, hiring on with the White and Swearington outfit near Big Spring in the early 1920s, accepted his fate with a shrug and a quip.

"He was a little bitty guy," remembered Ralph Davis, a fellow hand. "The foreman asked him, 'What kind of horse do you want, Fin?' And he said, 'Give me the worst SB you got, 'cause I know I'm gonna get him anyhow.'"

Generally, the boss dictated which horses would be in a cowboy's "mount," or string of reserved saddle stock. If a new hand was given an option, he usually wasted little time in scrutinizing the available animals. Still, looks could be deceiving.

With endurance at a premium on the rugged Hood Mendel Ranch west of Fort Stockton in the 1920s, every newcomer was offered a choice between two mules of vastly different temperaments.

"One of 'em would be kicking and pitching and running and fighting, and the other would stand just as docile as a lamb," recalled Olan George, a Mendel cowhand. "Invariably, the new hands would pick the little black one that seemed gentle. But when you stepped in that saddle, you went to a bronc-ridin'. When I went out there, she got me the first day. She threw every man. And the mule that did all the kicking, running, and squealing, you could throw that saddle on there and step on and she was just perfect. I think everybody got caught on that trick."

When William Broughton mounted up on his first morning with the Pool Ranch in Terry County about 1917, he had no reason to suspect any such mischief. After all, his horse was gentle and it responded well to the reins. Still, the sixteen-year-old cowhand's initiation was yet to come.

"When a calf would break out to run and you had to take out after him, this ol' horse would fall every time, tumble and throw me off," recounted Broughton. "And that went on all day, and those boys were just laughing and clapping their hands."

Only after bouncing around in the dirt from daylight till dark did the young cowboy realize that the boss had cut him out an animal infamous for its clumsiness.

Sometimes a new hand needed only to pay attention to avoid an eccentric or outlaw horse. Shorty Northcutt related an account in which a newcomer, as he mounted up, inquired about the name of his animal. Learning it, he soon found reason never to forget—the bronc proved wild and troublesome throughout a long, hard day. Nevertheless, when the boss cut him out the same horse the next morning and called it by a different name, the cowboy was none the wiser. Once more, the animal cold-jawed and pitched incessantly. On the third and fourth mornings, the boss continued to assign the unsuspecting cowboy the same troublesome bronc, which by now had a slew of aliases. Finally, the animal threw the newcomer hard to the alkali, eliciting howls of laughter.

"I'll bet," opined the boss, "he doggoned sure remembers that horse *this* time."

Occasionally a compassionate cowboy discreetly warned a new hand that mischief was afoot. When nineteen-year-old Leonard Hernandez signed on with a trail drive outfit late one evening about 1926, a veteran took him aside.

"We got a mean horse here," the man told him. "If you don't know it, the foreman will give you that horse and see how good a cowboy you are."

Hernandez's uncle, a top hand with the outfit, soon approached with his own warning. "Did they tell you about that horse?" he asked.

"Yeah, they told me about it," said the disheartened Hernandez.

"Well, I'll fix that horse. He's mean, but a man is meaner—a man is made to *handle* horses."

That night, Hernandez's uncle roped the bronc and struck it hard above the hoof with a rock. The next morning, the animal was too crippled for the boss to carry out his plan.

Usually, though, a cowboy was left to suffer the consequences of a prank involving a pitching horse.

"If you was a good rider," said Will Durham, a cowboy as early as 1900, "you could usually stay on him. If you weren't, you'd usually grab for the saddle horn and catch yourself in the seat of the britches about the time you hit the ground."

In such an event, a victim's fellow cowboys usually broke out in uproarious laughter.

Will Durham in 1989.

"That was part of the game," said Frank Derrick, who tumbled from the saddle his share of times. "But you'd *really* get hoorawed if you held on to the saddle or horn."

Pulling leather was bad enough, but to a fun-loving bunch of cowboys, there was something even more dishonorable.

"If you lost your hat, that was worse than getting throwed," said Joe Lambert. "They sure *would* hooraw you then."

In a cowboy's everyday life, nothing was any riskier than staying astride a cantankerous bronc through the demands of his profession. If he hadn't seen a rider killed—by fall, hoof, or dragging—he probably had heard plenty of such stories. For some cowhands, it was reason enough to refrain from certain pranks.

"You don't mess with a man's horse when he's on him—or off of him either one, if he catches you doing it," said Slim Vines.

Nevertheless, less-prudent cowhands persisted in encouraging another rider's horse to pitch, with seldom a thought to the ensuing danger.

"When I was about twelve years old, a boy and I were going along, driving these cattle [on a Mertzon-area ranch]," recalled Douglas Poage. "I had a rope tied to the saddle horn. He stuck a stick under my horse's tail and he kicked up real high and threw me off. I went right off down

Douglas Poage in 1990.

his right shoulder, and when my foot came over the saddle, it hung in that rope. It broke the horn string and the loop come out and looped around my spur rowel."

Suddenly the horse was off, dragging Poage at his hooves.

"He drug me about 400 yards," he recounted. "I didn't know what to think. I reached in my pocket to get my pocketknife and see if I could cut the rope, but I didn't have my pocketknife. This boy was coming along trying to catch the horse, and he was about even with me when my spur come off over my heel and I was loose. It didn't hurt me other than skin me up. We found my pocketknife laying on the ground right where he threw me."

For the sake of an innocent attempt at humor, young Poage had narrowly escaped a tragic fate to which a bronc could sentence a cowpuncher at any time. Indeed, even without inducement, horses both gentle and snaky could give cowboys plenty of close calls and innumerable chances to hooraw another rider.

Horsin' Around

When it came to an ornery horse, a cowboy's greatest challenge was not so much staying in the saddle as it was getting there in the first place. Seldom was a cowhand so vulnerable as when he tried to dig his foot in the stirrup, and many a bronc seized the opportunity to unleash its repertoire of tricks—spinning, bolting, pitching. Once astride such an uncooperative animal, a cowboy often avoided dismounting at all costs. Nevertheless, in trying to outsmart an outlaw, a horseman sometimes succeeded only in outsmarting himself.

When Walter Boren was a hand in the Pecos River country near present Crane in the late 1910s, he witnessed the misery one such bronc dealt a fellow cowboy on the Adobe Ranch.

"That horse was sure hard to get on," recalled Boren. "The ol' boy was riding along and wanted to urinate, so he thought he'd just urinate out between the fork of the saddle and save himself a lot of trouble. When he did, it went running down the horse's leg—and that ol' bronc throwed him anyway."

When cowboys gathered to chew the fat, they usually found the greatest humor in the unforeseen troubles a horse could spawn. Maybe it would be something as benign as a rider breaking a stiff hat brim while fanning a bucking animal—as Gaston Boykin once did after soaking his hat in a sugar-water solution—or as serious as a thrown cowboy executing a belly buster smack-dab into a bobcat. But among laughter-starved cowboys, such stories were sure to evoke a hearty response.

Although a cowhand took a lot of pride in his work, he generally didn't suffer from vanity. On the contrary, he savored the memory of every embarrassing episode and was quick to share it.

"One time I was riding an ol' horse that'd go to bucking if you even spit off of him," recounted Slim Vines. "Howard Hale and I were taking a bunch of cattle to a pasture, and that horse fell in two and I grabbed for the saddle horn and missed it. That ol' pony throwed me off and then just went out there two or three steps and stopped and looked back at me. Ol' Howard was laughing at me, but I went and got on again."

As Vines once more took position around the herd, Hale continued to hooraw him. "Slim," asked Hale, "what in the world happened?"

"I don't know. I was just riding along there and that booger fell in two and I grabbed for the saddle horn like *that*."

The instant Vines reenacted the scene, the bronc gave its own encore, unceremoniously dumping Vines to the alkali for the second time. Recalled Vines:

"Ol' Howard just liked to died laughing. From then on, every once in a while he'd say, 'Slim, what was it you did when that horse throwed you off?'"

When a cowboy lost his seat in the saddle, he never knew just what kind of humiliating fix awaited him. Sometimes, to his surprise, he might not even hit the ground.

Trying to rope wormy cattle in a pen on the Spade Ranch near Colorado City in the 1930s, Fred McClellan and Shorty Northcutt grew discontented with their mounts.

Fred McClellan and Ben Atwell at the old Spade Ranch corrals in the late 1920s or early 1930s. (courtesy, Fred McClellan)

"I was riding an ol' sorrel horse that wouldn't back or pull, and Fred couldn't get his ol' horse close enough to heel one of them wormies," remembered Northcutt. "Directly he got mad at him and went to jobbing his spurs. That ol' pony broke in two and carried him clear across the corral."

"That son-of-a-gun, he just got to bucking in a circle," noted McClellan. "I got over on one side of him and finally he just slung me loose."

Neither man would ever forget what happened to McClellan on his way down.

"His spurs and heels hung over the fence and ol' Fred just stood up on his head," said Northcutt.

When McClellan finally extricated himself from the predicament, Northcutt dismounted from his own troublesome bronc. Spying a nearby two-by-four, the two frustrated cowboys decided not to spoil their horses any further by sparing the rod.

"We was really working 'em over," recounted Northcutt. "Next morning [Spade manager Otto] Jones come to the wagon and ol' Coosie Jackson—the smart aleck—asked, 'Mr. Jones, y'all have some new horses out there this morning?' Jones said, 'I don't reckon. Why?' Coosie says, 'Well, I heard some boys hammering some out there yesterday afternoon.'"

One cowboy, uprooted from the saddle in a thicket near Eagle Pass one cold day in the 1920s, found an even more ignoble landing spot.

"We was rounding up steers and there was a lot of big old mesquite trees," remembered Leonard Hernandez, a fellow cowhand. "This fellow was wearing one of those heavy ducking jackets. He was following one of them steers with his horse on a run, and he must've ducked down when he seen a limb coming straight at him."

Although the cowboy avoided the crushing impact, his troubles were only beginning. With his head lowered, the jutting limb caught the exposed collar of his jacket and peeled him from the saddle. Left swinging like a pendulum to the snag's vice-like grip, the cowboy could only watch helplessly as his loping horse kept up its hard run and disappeared.

Not only had no one witnessed the mishap, but he was snared in such a way that he could neither seize a limb nor shed his jacket. Boots kicking, he dangled there like a hanged man a full night before searching cowhands rescued him.

Few tossed riders, though, ever found themselves in the straits Keith Dunn did one long-ago day on the U Ranch in Sterling County. Astride a gentle brown gelding called Ol' Britches, Dunn jumped a bobcat in the brush and gigged the horse in pursuit. Coming up behind the fleeing varmint, he kept Ol' Britches right on its tail long enough to pull a six-shooter and take aim between the horse's ears. Firing, he only creased the bobcat's neck and stunned it, while the sudden *blam!* startled Ol' Britches out of its wits.

"No question about it," recalled Little George McEntire of the U Ranch, "Ol' Britches unloaded him right there. Ol' Keith hit right on top of the bobcat—and the bobcat, halfway coming to and trying to get away, liked to tore him to pieces."

Draggings were seldom something to grin about, but ever so often there occurred one so comical that it demanded recounting for any cowpoke who needed a good laugh.

Upon hiring on with the Davidson outfit near Ozona in the early 1930s, greenhorn Tom Powers purchased a new saddle in which he took vainglorious pride.

"He was very particular with it," recalled his older brother Ted Powers. "He didn't want to get a scratch on it."

"The first time he rode it," remembered Bill Townsend, who cowboyed with the Powers brothers, "we started off down through the pasture and found a cow that needed doctoring [for screwworms]. That fresh leather wasn't stretched out, and when Tom roped this animal it jerked his saddle off. The cow started dragging it off and ol' Tom jumped up from the ground and got in that saddle. That cow went on down through the brush with him just a-ridin' it. Skinned him up all over his face and head, and later ol' Bill Grimmer asked, 'Well, Tom, why didn't you let that thing alone?' Tom told him, 'I just didn't want my new saddle going down through that brush.'"

With young Tom aspiring to be a bronc rider, his older brother cut him out a spirited gelding that would give him practical experience. After getting thrown and left afoot far out in the pasture a couple of times, Tom acquired a pair of bridle reins long enough to reach the ground and give him hope of hanging on to the animal. As Davidson hand Fat Alford rounded up on a mesa one morning, he happened to glance over the rimrock at the flat below.

"Fat saw Tom's horse hang his head and start bucking," recounted Ted Powers. "Tom got bucked off, but he held on to those bridle reins, and that horse was jumping back and forth over him. That horse was bucking all over Tom, but he wouldn't turn him loose."

Alford immediately wheeled his horse and picked his way down to the flat, only to find Tom astride the animal again.

"Tom," he admonished, "if that son-of-a-gun starts to buck all over you like that, don't hold on to him—he could hurt you."

"But I don't want him running off with my new saddle," retorted Tom, stroking the still-immaculate leather.

At noon, the two cowhands rode back to the chuck wagon and unsaddled their tired horses. When Tom gingerly laid his saddle on a blanket rather than on the ground, Alford decided enough was enough. To the kid's dismay, Alford seized the saddle and fled, dragging it through rocks and thorns until it bore the undeniable scars of a top hand's kack. Tom, completely unnerved, choused the older cowhand with rocks, but the tickled Alford dodged and finally hung the saddle on a fence.

As Tom rushed up to inspect the damage, Alford stifled his laughter long enough to give him a little advice:

"You'll never amount to anything if you're afraid you're going to get that thing skinned up a little. Get some skinned places on it and you *might* make a cowboy some day."

If a cowboy ever got hopelessly hung to a runaway horse and dragged, he only had three chances—someone had to cut the animal off, someone had to shoot it, or the desperate victim somehow had to regain the saddle. Otherwise, as a lot of lonely graves bore witness, a stump or jutting rock might lay in wait, or, even worse, the dragged cowhand might face hours of torture that could render his corpse unrecognizable.

It was exactly those options that came into play when the Whitehead outfit's lone black cowboy got hung to a horse on a long-ago roundup drive through the cedary hills near Kerrville. Respected for his horse-breaking abilities, the black cowhand nevertheless had never been fully accepted into the cowboys' fraternity, for such was the social fabric of the day. Therefore, when he suddenly found himself in trouble, he had reason to doubt the resolve of his companions to save his life.

"One man was carrying a 30-30 in his saddle for coyotes," related Billy Rankin, who heard the story in the late 1920s or early 1930s. "When this horse threwed that Negro off, he hung his foot in the stirrup. The horse was running, and old man Whitehead hollered to the boy with the gun, '*Shoot him! Shoot him! Shoot him!*'"

As the cowboy shouldered the rifle and took aim, he suddenly held his fire. Incredibly, the black cowhand had managed to seize the stirrup, and now he was pulling himself up along the animal's rib cage. Moments later, he regained the saddle to pull rein, and as he wheeled the horse, he found every cowhand's mouth agape.

"How in the world did you ever crawl back on that bronc?" asked one disbelieving cowboy. "I've never seen anything like it!"

"Well," said the black cowhand, dusting himself off, "when Mr. Whitehead said 'Shoot him!,' I knowed he didn't mean that horse."

It wasn't the only time a horse mishap was most memorable for what the victim had to say.

"I remember one ol' boy that got bucked off," said Slim Vines. "Just as soon as the horse threw him off, the animal quit bucking. Somebody asked him, 'How come you to get bucked off?' The ol' boy said, 'Well, I rode him till he made that last jump. If he hadn't've made that last jump, I'd still be a-ridin' him.'"

Famous humorist Will Rogers, working a long-ago roundup on the Mashed O near Earth, also was quick with a quip. Roping a calf and dragging it to the branding fire, he let his horse (which bore a Mashed O brand) step over the rope with its hind foot.

"That horse pitched him off on his hip," recalled John Murrell of the Mashed O. "He got up, kinda shook himself, and said, 'I thought I was gonna ride him till I saw that Mashed O fly off of him.'"

Howard Capps, charged with breaking a two-year-old outlaw horse named Wampus on the Davidson Ranch near Ozona in 1935, didn't find much to joke about after the animal pitched him off repeatedly in a cattle pen oozing with manure. Making his way to the nearest telephone, he called owner Joe Davidson in Ozona.

"Joe," he said, "I'm gonna quit. I want to come to town. I want you to come down and get me."

"What's the matter, Howard?" asked Davidson.

"I'm getting tired of rolling around in this cow dung," Capps replied.

A horse wreck often addled a cowboy for a spell, and his tangled tongue was notorious for blurting a memorable line when someone rushed up to help.

Arliss Cotton, knocked silly in a horse fall on the Spade Ranch long ago, looked up at the hovering Shorty Northcutt and had only one thing to say: "Which a-way is north? Which a-way is north?"

Eidson Ranch cowhand Marvin Hooper, stunned when his horse fell over backwards with him near Penwell in the early 1930s, began to regain his senses only after his wife snatched up his hat, filled it with water, and splashed him full in the face. Moaning and writhing from a broken shoulder as he looked up, his every thought suddenly was on nothing but the dripping brim in his wife's hand.

"Damn!" he exclaimed. "You've ruined my new hat!"

Maybe no one laughed at the time, but Hooper wouldn't be the last cowboy to find out that an enduring bit of humor can sometimes rise from the ashes of misfortune.

Hoorawing
Day and Night

At a dollar a day, a cowboy of the early 1900s set a standard against which many American workers paled.

"A cowboy was a fellow that had a lot of self-respect and pride about his work and, if he was sober, conducted himself properly," noted Tom Blasingame. "He didn't hide in back of nobody, and he had certain rules—saddle manners, they called it. Back then, they was pretty much like a man ought to be."

But the very fact that a cowboy was almost invariably hard-working, dedicated, and reliable made him vulnerable to a classic prank: at the behest of the boss, he would set out to retrieve a certain item—a bottle of screwworm medicine maybe, or a forgotten quirt or pair of leggings. After a grueling ride across a sprawling pasture, it was plenty embarrassing to realize that the objective of his quest was about as real as a tow sack full of Texas snipe.

If anything was downright disheartening to such a loyal ranch hand, it was to try to carry out some assigned chore with top-hand efficiency, only to get waylaid by mischief or pull some greenhorn stunt. Even worse, he might let himself get caught unawares in a situation that would have made even a city boy turn red.

Marvin Hooper knew the feeling, for the hard-riding cowboy once fell prey to something as seemingly innocuous as a walking tub of lard. It began one morning in the early 1930s when he pulled rein at Sand Windmill, ten miles from the Eidson Ranch headquarters near Penwell. Securing his horse in an outlying corral, he climbed the tower to grease the mill.

"When I was up on top of that windmill," Hooper recalled, "an old wild sow and a bunch of little pigs come up. I got through greasing the windmill and started to come down, and when I got pretty close to the bottom, here come that old sow just a-snortin'. All I could do was go back up. That was along about nine o'clock in the morning. And when the sun went down, I was still a-settin' up on that windmill. A little after sundown, that old sow finally got them pigs and went on."

Embarrassed at spending the entire day in such ignoble fashion, Hooper was less than reassured when, on the ride back to headquarters, he met up with Al Long, who had come in search.

"Hooper," asked the cowhand, studying his features in the shadows, "where you been all day?"

"Treed in that windmill," Hooper admitted sheepishly.

There were some things a cowboy could never anticipate, but even if he did plan for an adverse condition, his fellow cowhands might deem him *too* prepared and take steps to change matters.

Readying to ride out and work cattle in southwest Texas one morning, Leonard Hernandez cast a wary glance at the cloudless sky. "It's gonna rain, boys," he warned. "I'm gonna take my raincoat with me."

"Aaah, you're crazy," replied one of the hands. "Who told you it was gonna rain?"

"Nobody, but I tell you, it's gonna rain this evening."

To a steady hoorawing, Hernandez took up his raincoat and tied it on the back of his saddle. Sure enough, about three o'clock that afternoon a thunderhead began to rise over the horizon. Recounted Hernandez:

"Boy, it really started lightning and raining. Just as I untied my raincoat, two of them boys got together, one on one side and the other on the other side, and ripped my coat in two. 'Now!' they told me. 'Get wet like the rest of us!'"

When a cowboy day-herded around a water hole on a hot afternoon, he occasionally grabbed a quick siesta while the cattle were at ease. Upon awakening, he might find his horse missing and the other cowhands professing ignorance. To their hooraws, he might traipse around under the blazing sun for long minutes before stumbling upon his hidden mount.

A cowboy was no less a target when he rode pasture alone. Between doctoring wormy cattle and checking float valves and fences, he sometimes paused in a shady spot for a brief snooze. Cyclone Ellis, riding a T Half Circle pasture in Sutton County one long-ago summer, came upon a big live oak mott and couldn't resist the temptation. Tying his horse, he made a pallet of his leggings and was soon fast asleep. Little did he know that his boss, Willie Wilkinson, was aware of his weakness for siestas and had trailed him to the very spot.

Caught red-handed in an undeniable nap, Ellis was quick to defend himself. "I wasn't gonna sleep but about fifteen minutes—I never do. I just have to have about fifteen minutes after dinner."

A couple of days later, Wilkinson again trailed his siesta-prone cowhand across the pasture.

"Sure enough," recounted Ted Powers, who heard the story from Wilkinson, "Cyclone Ellis pulled under a big live oak thicket, tied his horse, pulled his chaps off, and laid down on 'em. Willie Wilkinson eased up there, tied his own horse, pulled off his chaps, and laid down beside him. He was gonna lay there and catch him when he woke up. Meantime, Willie went to sleep himself and he didn't wake up till nearly sundown and Cyclone was long gone."

When a cowboy rode back to the line shack or bunkhouse for the night, he gained little reprieve from practical jokers. If a fellow was still a little green, a couple of hands might show him the magic coat sleeve.

"Back in those days," remembered Fred McClellan, "they had those big ol' sheepskin coats. They'd hold this sleeve up and tell some ol' green kid, 'Look through this sleeve and you'll see some magical things.' Of course, when he did, somebody would have a cup of cold water and pour it right down in his face."

Tenderfoot or not, a cowboy was always subject to developing boils on his backside. "You always get them ol' saddle sores when you first start riding hard again all day," noted Charlie Drennan. "Boy, they get to itching."

When one young cowhand came riding in gingerly and complained of his inability to sit, Drennan was quick to recommend caustic balsam, a horse salve, as a sure-fire cure. After the other cowboys also praised its medicinal qualities, the suffering greenhorn stripped and applied the ointment. Figuratively set afire, the kid had to dash out through the night and find the water trough with his bare bottom.

Seldom did a cowboy relish washing dishes; indeed, he was always on the lookout for a way to avoid this necessary, but demeaning, task. As Steve Armentrout heard the story, one cowhand found an efficient, although somewhat unsanitary, solution to the dilemma.

"This ol' boy was staying back at the ranch, and after these guys come in and ate, he just set the dishes out back for the two hounds," Armentrout recounted. "Then the boss come along, 'Got anything left for dinner?'

"'Yeah,' the ol' boy says.

"'Got any plates?'

"'Yeah.'

"'They clean?'

"'Yeah, just as clean as ol' Bob and Tom can lick 'em.'"

Another way to escape dishwashing duty was by pawning the lowly task off on a trusting cowhand through trickery. One such method was known as "Honest John."

"When a new guy come, you'd play a game of Honest John," recalled Gaston Boykin, who cowboyed in the Ozona country. "You'd put a number seven on every slip of paper, put it all in a hat, and we'd draw after every meal. Whoever got number seven had to wash dishes. Of course, only Honest John would admit he had it, even though the others had it too. We kept one kid washing dishes for several days before he ever caught on."

Gaston Boykin about 1923 on the Boykin Ranch in Comanche County. (courtesy, Gaston Boykin)

Another favorite trick was to convince a wide-eyed kid that a crazy man was on the prowl. Usually, the conspirators began by planting a suggestion in the dupe's mind.

"Have you been a-noticin' ol' Arthur Judkins lately?" a cowboy asked a long-ago greenhorn on the McElroy Ranch near Crane. "There's something the matter with him."

Shortly afterward, as they gathered for supper, the kid looked up to see Judkins foaming at the mouth. Shrinking from the mad-dog-of-a-cowboy, the shaken greenhorn never suspected that Judkins had slipped a bar of soap in his mouth.

Similarly, Claude Owens, sharing a Crockett County ranch house with Shorty Jones long ago, confided in his naive companion that he was subject to "spells."

"I told him I was pretty loco and he believed it," Owens recalled. "One night he and I were there by ourselves and I jumped up and run out of the house, just kinda acting crazy, and he took after me. He caught me way down the road and tried to pick me up and carry me back. The next morning, he began to tell me what all had happened. I said, 'Just don't tell my folks—I don't want them to send me back down to San Antonio and the doctors again.' I had him taking pretty good care of me."

On the Miller spread twenty-five miles south of Ozona, cowhands conspired in the 1920s to scare a tenderfoot fresh out of East Texas.

"He was a good kid, but he was windy," remembered Boykin. "So we got to telling him for a week about an old wild man that lived up in the canyon there. Then one day I went up there and I hid my horse. I made me some hair out of a tow sack and waited until dusk. I pulled off my shirt and started turning over rocks, making out like I was eating bugs."

Meanwhile the boss and his sons, who were part of the conspiracy, ventured up the canyon with the greenhorn. En route, they agreed that, if the wild man attacked, they would split up so that at least some of them might escape. Recounted Boykin:

I waited until they got within about fifty yards of me and I jerked up my shotgun and started shooting over their heads. They began to split and run in different directions. I run and jumped on my horse and circled around and got home fast as I could, about three-quarters of a mile. I unsaddled the horse right quick, turned him loose, put the saddle up, and went to the house.

I was there talking to the owner's wife, and I heard this boy hit a fence over there two or three hundred yards away. Then we could hear his footsteps, and hear him hit another fence and then another. When he come to the yard fence, he just dove over and landed on his belly. He lay there panting, and after awhile he looked up and said, "Mrs. Miller, you've been wanting to reduce—you oughta go up there and see that old wild man! I bet I lost fifteen pounds!"

Out in a wagon camp, cowboys found even more opportunities to get a chuckle at the expense of a "tenderfootin'" newcomer. As dark fell and the shadows crept close to the campfire, they might warn him that they could expect gunfire at any moment. Or, if the outfit didn't prohibit card playing, a couple of cowhands might put on a show for the gullible kid.

"I've seen a couple of fellows get in a poker game and lay their six-shooters down there by the side of 'em," recalled Tom Blasingame, who cowboyed from Texas to

California. "Directly, they'd have a falling out, you know, and go to cussing one another. Then they'd grab them six-shooters and go to shooting. Of course, they was careful not to hit nobody, but that tenderfoot—so damned ignorant and green—would break and run. They'd have a lot of fun that away. Maybe shoot over his head. One time, one of 'em laid out all night long."

With beans a staple of a cowhand's diet, it was inevitable that a pebble would occasionally find its way into the pot. Still, given the camp cook's legendary cantankerousness, a dissatisfied cowboy had to broach the subject with kid gloves or get his neck wrung. Even if the cook did agree to cull the beans more carefully next time, a cowhand might get a mischievous glint in his eye.

"There was a kid that worked [in the Panhandle] for a short time who'd always pick up a little handful of pebbles," recalled Frank Derrick. "After he got his helping of beans, he'd drop those rocks in the bean pot for the ones behind. Of course, they'd cuss the cook about it."

Beans were notorious for their flatulent properties, and a lot of gassy cowboys paid a price for their campfire indiscretions.

"When we'd be sitting around camp and eating," recalled William Broughton, "if you broke wind, you had to say, 'One two three, my [gas] is free.' If you didn't, they'd take a skillet and give you licks with it."

This mock penance, sometimes administered with chaps as the victim lay across a bedroll or the wagon tongue, occasionally was preceded by a kangaroo court.

"If you didn't want to take the punishment, you could appoint one of the other hands to defend you," noted Fred McClellan. "But if they convicted you, they'd give you about twenty licks with leggings. You could choose the man to administer the punishment, but you just had to take it."

"It was all in fun," observed Tom Blasingame, "but that fellow that had them chaps, he'd bear down on it, 'cause he figured he might get chapped too later on."

When night fell on a cow camp and it came time to "sack 'em in," pranksters seemed to hit their stride. If they looked up from their lumpy bedrolls to see a fellow sprawled on a comfortable cot, they might ease out of bed, grab their ropes, and secure him to its frame. Or, as Bud Mayes recalled, they might swoop down on a sleeping tenderfoot, tie him up in his bedding, and hang him on a fence post.

But the most insidious form of wagon camp humor involved slipping an unpleasant item in a cowboy's bedding.

"You'd roll your bed out, and if you was gonna be there again that night, you'd just leave it laying out," recalled Walton Poage. "They might stick a turtle in there. For some ol' boy they didn't like, it might be a little worse."

Sometimes, even a well-liked cowboy could find an especially unwelcome guest sharing his covers.

"In about '18 on the Pool Ranch north of Brownfield, I crawled in my bed on the ground and didn't think anything about it," remembered Broughton. "Gosh-a-mighty, I felt something squirming against my leg and I come out of there really a-cussin'. It was a live rat snake, and all these cowboys began laughing. I knew darned well that they'd put that damned snake in there."

Walton Poage at Stiles in the mid-1940s.

Equally revolting in a fellow's bedding was a water dog, or salamander.

"Used to, you'd camp around them ol' earthen tanks," recalled Joe Lambert. "If it rained, them things would just crawl. Somebody'd get out there and catch one of 'em after we nearly all got to sleep. We wore them BVDs, and he'd turn that thing loose in bed with you and it'd go to crawling on you. They was just as cold as ice. You'd know what it was, but I'll guarantee you, you'd come out of bed fast."

Other favorites earmarked for a cowhand's bedding were a cactus, a cow pile, or a dead creature such as a rat. However, there was a fine line between mischief and malice sometimes, and a prankster always had to be sure the victim knew the difference.

Joe Lambert in 1989.

"Sometimes a prank would cause trouble," admitted Frank Derrick. "But you always picked on somebody that you thought you could handle."

One ill-advised prank, which reportedly occurred near Brady about 1916, served as a warning to some cowboys to refrain from bedtime foolishness.

"This guy told a fellow, 'I'm gonna pull a prank on you,'" said Lewis Doran, recounting the version he heard through the cowboy grapevine. "The other ol' boy said, 'You better not, 'cause I don't go for that.' Sure enough, the ol' boy found a snake in his bed. He had his six-shooter laying there. He knew the one that done it, so he pulled his six-shooter and shot him down right there. That stopped all that stuff—you don't want nobody throwing a snake in your bed."

Rarely did a duped cowboy resort to violence, much less to shooting the perpetrator. His temper might flare for a moment, but he usually accepted his role as the butt of a practical joke in the spirit of good fun. Indeed, it presented a golden opportunity, for a cowboy delighted in good-natured payback.

Headed back to the Six-Mile Ranch near Fort McKavett about 1920 after a cattle drive through Central Texas, drovers began hoorawing sixteen-year-old cowhand Willard Renfro, who proceeded to spur his horse into flight. Pursuing, the cowboys roped his animal, forcing Renfro to pull rein. When he dismounted, someone slapped his horse on the rump and the gelding fled.

Not content with setting Renfro afoot, Oran Slaughter seized a catch rope and set his sights squarely on the young cowboy.

"He was going to rope *me*," recalled Renfro, who had his own coiled lariat in hand. "I ducked and got his rope, and he made a run on it—he was going to jerk it out of my grasp. But I tied it around a little ol' mesquite tree there real quick. When he hit the end of that rope, it jerked his horse down."

Mounting up again, the embarrassed Slaughter once more came at Renfro with loop swinging, only to find Renfro beating him to the punch.

"I took my rope and threw it, and caught his horse around the neck," remembered Renfro. "I sat down on it and held it; his horse was about to fall over backwards with me. He was hollering and cussing and raising hell: 'Turn that rope loose! You're gonna break my horse's neck—me too!' I said, 'Hell, you didn't think about *me* when you was pulling on *me*, did you?'"

The possibility of retaliation was seldom foremost in a cowboy's mind when he conceived a practical joke, but when it came, it often was memorable. As in Renfro's case, it could sometimes be blunt and rowdy.

On the X Ranch near Kent in the early 1920s, Jack Pate, a slight 130-pounder, slipped up behind 212-pound Doc Kennedy on a pier at an earthen tank.

"It was in December and, of course, the water was cold," recounted Pate. "He stooped over to dip up a bucket of water, and I just gave him a push with my foot. I'd always been able to outrun him till then. He caught me going down a draw full of cockleburs. My hair was long, and he got me down and just rubbed them cockleburs in my hair. He really gave me a massaging."

Soon afterward, the two cowboys reversed roles. Catching Pate afoot, the mounted Kennedy roped him like a calf. When the horse instinctively backed up to tighten the hold, Pate suddenly became an acrobat, to Kennedy's delight. "He turned me over about three or four somer-sets," recalled Pate.

Biding his time, Pate seized upon an idea for retaliation a few mornings later when he watched Kennedy walk away through an open-gap gate.

"I tied baling wire about six inches from the ground across there," he remembered. "Just as he came back, I threw a stewer of water on him, and he charged me. He hit that wire and I let him down just as hard as he did me. That's the way we played."

Lonnie Griffith, a young cowboy on his stepfather's ranch in Borden County in the 1910s, also knew how to play a rough game of payback. He had good reason to learn, for cowhand Tom Hudson had dealt him a lot of misery over the years.

"He was an ornery son-of-a-gun; don't think he wasn't," Griffith noted. "He quirted me a-many a time with a big quirt. But we didn't tell on him, and anything we done to him, he didn't tell on us."

Finding Hudson approaching one day with his horse in a lope, Griffith and another young hand saw a chance for revenge.

"We was riding along in the pasture right side-by-side and I handed the kid the end of my rope," recounted Griffith. "Ol' Tom thought he was gonna run past us, but just before he got to us, we just spread out with that rope on our saddle horns. It caught him right on the belly and jerked him off his damned horse. I tell you, we had to stay away from him for quite a while, 'cause he'd just whip the devil out of us."

Finding Hudson an unwelcome houseguest one night, Griffith and his partner conspired to make his stay as unpleasant as possible. While Hudson was preoccupied with Griffith's folks and the charms of a visiting schoolmarm, the two cowhands sneaked upstairs into the man's bedroom.

"We pulled the sheet back and laid a great big bur under the sheet," remembered Griffith. "Boy, that durned thing was just full of stickers."

Slipping out the window and taking position on the ledge, Griffith and his accomplice waited in the dark.

"Tom come up there and pulled off his clothes, and when he fell back on that bed, you could've heard him yell five miles," Griffith narrated. "Dad come running in there to see what was wrong with him, and he caught that ol' sheet and just jerked it off of ol' Tom and it liked to killed him. I bet you he had a thousand little ol' blood spots all over his back."

Payback could also be subtle and creative. On a long-ago drive to Barnhart, a trail outfit turned a herd into a trap for the night. Catching Gaston Boykin and another

Gaston Boykin in 1989.

cowhand momentarily afoot, the mounted cowboys rode away with their horses and left them to trudge back to camp through a pouring rain. Arriving wet and tired, the victims stoically endured the hooraws, but when dark fell, they carried out a plan they had carefully devised across two miles of muddy pasture.

"We got their alarm clock and fixed it where it'd go off at 11 P.M., but it'd show 3 A.M., the time they was going to get up," remembered Boykin. "When it went off, they got up, cooked their breakfast and ate, and sat up all night—and we slept."

Long ago on the SMS Ranch on the Texas South Plains, where a cowboy's smoke of choice was Prince Albert, a hand named Jeff Kennedy hatched a fiendish—and highly ingenious—mode of retaliation for the impish heist of his tobacco tin. A classic instance of prank, payback, and attempted counter-payback, the episode illustrated the lengths to which a cowhand would go in search of a laugh.

"These boys would lay down on their bedroll, set this pocket-sized tobacco tin down beside their bed, and smoke and talk," recounted Joe Lambert. "One ol' boy would catch 'em all asleep, go over and take somebody else's can, and set his nearly empty one down in its place."

Kennedy, once he determined what was happening, didn't take kindly to the prank. Related Lambert:

> Jeff had his pistol. He pulled a bullet out of it and took that powder and just spread it over the tobacco in his Prince Albert can. In the night, Jeff was about half awake, and he saw this ol' boy reach over there and get his [Jeff's] can and set his own down there in its place. The next morning, the ol'

boy rolled himself a cigarette and that thing went off and liked to have blown his head off.

Surmising what had happened, the prankster-turned-victim decided to exact revenge. Sprinkling gunpowder over his own tobacco, he switched tins with Kennedy again a couple of nights later. Returning to bed with a grin, the cowhand drifted off to sleep and waited for the morning fireworks. Little did he realize that Kennedy had been awake through the whole shenanigan.

Sitting up in bed the next morning, the cowhand eyed the waking Kennedy and waited for him to roll a cigarette. Snickering in anticipation, the unwitting prankster struck a match on his boot and cupped the flame to his own first smoke.

At the last instant, he glanced up and caught Kennedy's devilish grin, then the prankster's cigarette exploded like a 12-gauge shotgun. Only then, spitting gun smoke and wiping at his powder-blackened face, did he realize what all the howling cowboys already seemed to know.

During the night, Kennedy had swapped cans yet again.

Trail's End

On December 30, 1989, Tom Blasingame, who lived a cowboy's life and met a cowboy's death, was buried a cowboy's way.

With his riderless horse breaking trail and his empty boots swinging in the stirrups, a procession which included eight mounted ranch hands carried him one last time across a sprawling land he had ridden for three-quarters of a century. Deep in his beloved Palo Duro Canyon, they laid him to rest in the almost-forgotten JA cemetery with the same simple dignity with which he had lived his life.

"Look at my country: no farms or nothing," he had said only months before, with a sweep of his arm to the reddish folds of the Palo Duro bluffs. "To get to ride in a cattle country and work cattle...that's my life."

But even while choosing the same unchiseled epitaph as Lonnie Griffith and almost every other old-time cowhand—*My Life Was in the Saddle*—Blasingame also dwelled on their common sense of loss. Little by little, the encroachment of civilization had chipped away at a cowboy's place until, inasmuch as the old ways were concerned, the world had little need for men of their kind.

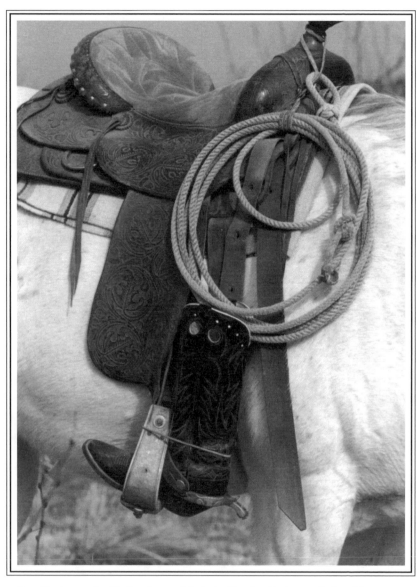

Tom Blasingame's riderless horse. (photo by Skeeter Hagler, as featured in *Persimmon Hill Magazine*)

"I didn't see much of that frontier life after them trucks and things come along," Blasingame reflected with almost mournful regret. "It was altogether different them old days. Seems like the people were different than they are now. They was friendly, big-hearted. I tell you, people was *happy* them days. They can say what they want to about these modern times; by gosh, people was happier then than they are now. Seems like they enjoyed each other's company when we *did* meet. Hell, now it's altogether different."

Then, with a cowboy's way, Blasingame's voice dropped and he cut to the heart of the matter, one last lament for a way of life that was no more.

"I wish them old days was back here again—the best years of my life was then, you know. But I can tell you this: that time's gone... and we'll never see it again."

Nor will the world again see cowboys of his kind, or of Griffith's, or of their seventy-four partners' in the Last-of-a-Breed Outfit. Through history, past legend, and on into destiny, they cut an enduring trace that still threads its way onward as far as the eye can see. Perhaps at trail's end, in some golden pasture where time never ends, they will ride yet again.

The
Last-of-a-Breed
Outfit

Seventy-six cowboys who would do to ride the river with:

ALEXANDER, HEWITT. Interviewed 16 October
1990 by telephone, Jasper.

Alexander was born August 30, 1909, and began working cattle in Louisiana at a young age. His Texas
cowboying experience began in the early 1930s, when he
signed on with a ranch near San Angelo. In the mid-1930s,
he drove several herds of cattle to San Angelo from the Joe
Meyers spread ten miles south of Vancourt. "I rode a horse
a-many a mile and never got hurt," he noted. He later
managed ranches near Jasper and Kirbyville.

ARMENTROUT, STEVE "SLIM." Interviewed 1
September 1989, Fort Stockton.

"To this day," reflected Armentrout as he neared
eighty, "if I had my choice, I'd ride a horse before I would
an automobile. There's just something about it that draws
you, if you love horses. And I did." Born east of Eldorado
February 8, probably in 1911 (there is some uncertainty
about the year), he helped his father do ranch work in the

Eldorado area as a youngster. In 1931 or 1932, shortly after marrying, he hired out to Bob's Creek Ranch in Sterling County. Later in the 1930s, he cowboyed in the Ozona region for ranches such as the 7N, situated along present Interstate 10 at a point twenty to twenty-five miles west of Ozona. He also worked for the E-2 outfit on the Schleicher-Crockett county line and for T. A. Kincaid in Upton County.

ARROTT, CLARENCE. Interviewed 13 October 1990 by telephone, Bronte.

Arrott was born in 1901 in Cherokee and began working cattle at age five. In 1907 he helped his father drive a small bunch of cattle from Cherokee to Eldorado. By age sixteen Arrott was cowboying on a thirty-section ranch his father had taken up about twenty-five miles south of Marathon. As a "stray man" for the Arrott Ranch, he worked roundup with the Gage outfit in the Big Bend. "You'd have to get up of a morning at four o'clock and catch your horse out of the bunch in a rope corral," he remembered. "A lot of times, I've had to lay down on my stomach nearly to tell which horse was mine [by the markings on its legs]." Arrott also cowboyed in the Ozona and Sheffield regions.

BAKER, LOUIS. Interviewed 14 February 1990, Bronte.

Born March 15, 1900, in Coke County, Baker grew up on a Coke County farm and was hiring out to nearby ranches by age ten. By 1921 he was punching cattle full time. Over the next several years, he cowboyed for outfits near Orient, Mertzon, and Barnhart, as well as in Reeves

County and in Oklahoma. "There's two things that you learned when you were cowboying—to tell the truth and not be trying to lay something off on somebody else," he said. "If them ol' cowboys caught one a-lyin', they'd beat the devil out of him." Baker married in 1926.

BEAUCHAMP, MARVIN. Interviewed 8 September 1989, Midland.

Beauchamp was born August 12, 1907, in Beckville and moved with his family to a homestead at Judkins (two miles west of Penwell) in 1908. He began cowboying in 1930 for Henry Comings on a twenty-five-section ranch twenty-five miles northwest of Odessa. He later punched cattle for Tom

Marvin Beauchamp in his cowboying days. (courtesy, Ann Hicks)

Nance on a twenty-section ranch thirty-five miles north of Midland, as well as for Roy Parks on the Estes place south of present Midland International Airport. In 1933 he began cowboying for Parks and Foy Proctor on a twenty-five-section ranch near Albany. In the mid-1930s, he worked on Proctor's sheep ranch west of Garden City. Although romanticized in literature and cinema, the cowboy life had its drudgery at times, he noted. "When you hook up a couple of horses to a wagon and throw a few posts and a little wire on it and go around and fix fence, it's not too glamorous," he said. He eventually became a fireman in Midland, serving in a volunteer capacity from 1936 to 1947 and as a paid fireman with Midland Fire Department from 1947 to 1973. Beauchamp died November 18, 1994, in Midland.

BLASINGAME, TOM. Interviewed 26 July 1989, JA Ranch, Armstrong County.

Born February 12, 1898, in Waxahachie, Blasingame moved with his family in 1901 to what is now southwest Oklahoma. By age three, he already was helping his father work cattle. Although Blasingame and his family soon relocated to the Dumas-Stratford area of Texas, by the time he was six they had again settled in present Oklahoma, where he helped drive herds as a young cowhand. In 1916 he signed on with the giant JA Ranch in Palo Duro Canyon in the Texas Panhandle. The next eighteen years saw him working for numerous big outfits, including the Matador; the Bell in New Mexico; the Double Circle, Chiricahua, Cross S, and 5L in Arizona; and the Circle 7 in California. "I liked to be a-horseback and I liked the big open country," he said. "I was kind of like a natural-born athlete like Babe Ruth, who never did want to do nothing else but play ball. That's the same way I was about cowboying." Blasingame met his wife-to-be at a dance at the JA in 1933 and married at the age of thirty-five. In 1934 he returned to the JA, where he continued to cowboy out of remote line camps until his death on the range at age ninety-one on December 27, 1989.

BOREN, WALTER. Interviewed 8 August 1990, Post.

Boren was born September 9, 1900, on the Jones-Fisher county line. He began helping his father do ranch work as a young boy on the family homestead four miles east of Justiceburg. Soon he was "neighboring" at nearby ranches, and by age fifteen he was hiring out. He made his first trail drive about 1915 from the OS Ranch near Post to Crosby County. During the drouth of 1916-1918, he cowboyed briefly in Oklahoma and then signed on with W. N.

Walter Boren in 1990.

Waddell at the Adobe Ranch near the Pecos River twenty miles south of present-day Crane. He later participated in a cattle drive from present Big Lake to a ranch near Fort Stockton. After marrying, he worked for an oil company. Even as he neared ninety, the memories of the broncs he had straddled as a young cowhand remained strong. "Whenever you got on one," he said, "you'd better screw down, because he'd start pitching."

BOYKIN, GASTON. Interviewed 13 September 1989, Comanche.

Boykin was born May 20, 1906, in Comanche County, where he grew up on a stock farm and broke his first horse at age thirteen. "I loved horses better than everything in the world," he remembered. When he was eighteen, he signed on with the Joe Montgomery Ranch in the Glass Mountains of West Texas. Soon afterward, he began punching cattle in the Ozona country, where he worked for several outfits until venturing to the 89,000-acre Shanghai Pierce Ranch near El Campo about 1939. Through it all, he came to understand the character of the typical cowboy. "When I was twenty-two, I was on one outfit where there wasn't a member of the church except myself," he recalled. "But they had their code of ethics and they'd be honest. They might cuss, but they wouldn't lie and wouldn't steal." After military service during World War II, Boykin returned to Comanche County and married in 1948. He served as Comanche County sheriff from 1946 to 1952 and from 1964 to 1976.

BRICE, LEE LOYD. Interviewed 13 August 1990, Ector County.

Born August 14, 1909, in Winters, Brice lived in Houston during World War I and later in Winters and Littlefield. He worked in the oil fields near the tent city of Crane in the mid-1920s and took up cowboying on the Bill Anderson ranch about fifteen miles north of Lovington, New Mexico, in the fall of 1929. "That was during a drouth and they was losing a lot of cattle," remembered Brice. "The cattle was getting poor, and they'd get down and couldn't get up. You'd have to haul feed to 'em. But a lot of 'em would stumble and fall and right there they'd die." In 1930, after a brief stint with the Gravy Fields outfit east of Tatum, New Mexico, he hired on with a 200-section spread

Lee Brice in 1990.

on the caprock west of Tatum. He later worked for the fifty-section Bunk Ship spread near Lovington, and the fifteen-section Jake McClure outfit fifteen miles west of Lovington.

BROUGHTON, WILLIAM EARNEST. Interviewed 23 February 1990 by telephone, Kimble County.

Broughton was born May 21, 1901, in Mitchell County, where his father ranched. He took up cowboying as a youngster on his father's ten-section spread near Gomez in Terry County. By age sixteen he began hiring out, first to the Albert McFall Ranch at Datil, New Mexico. He later worked for Bill Pool in Terry County and for Big Tree Hudson about thirty miles west of Portales, New Mexico. While riding night guard on cattle drives, he soothed the restless animals with a song he had composed. "I will tell you the work a cowboy has to do," he sang. "They brand and earmark and stand the guard too. To keep the herd from running, stampeding far and wide, it takes a cowboy's whistle, while riding by their side." Finally pulling off his leggings, he pinned on a badge in 1948 and served eight years as Ector County sheriff.

CALCOTE, BOB. Interviewed 14 October 1990 by telephone, Midkiff.

Born November 8, 1903, in Schleicher County, he first began hiring out as a cowhand about 1918 on the Henderson Ranch about fifteen miles east of Eldorado. He worked for the Homer Tippett outfit in the Pecos River country in the mid-1920s and on an Irion County spread in the early 1930s. Along the way, he rode his share of salty broncs.

"I've seen a lot of mean ones," he noted, "but I never did see too many that was smart." Calcote died May 15, 1993, in Midland.

CAUBLE, JACK. Interviewed 13 October 1990 by telephone, Vega.

Cauble was born October 27, 1906, in Albany, where his father and grandfather ranched. As a youngster of seven or so, he already was helping out on the spreads. He began hiring out at about age seventeen. He later cowboyed on Park Springs Ranch between the New Mexico cities of Las Vegas and Santa Rosa, at the Indio Ranch near Eagle Pass, and at ranches near Albany, Channing, and Vega, respectively. "Screwworms were awfully bad when I was at Eagle Pass back in the '30s," he recounted. "One morning, an ol' boy went to get his saddle blanket, and it was so dirty and nasty that even it had maggots." At the time of the interview, Cauble was still dayworking horseback for the Mansfield Ranch eleven miles north of Vega.

COGGINS, OTIS D. Interviewed 3 March 1990, Alpine.

Born June 16, 1902, in Frio County, Coggins began cowboying at about age eight with his grandfather, who ranched approximately fifty miles south of San Antonio. Coggins began hiring out by age fifteen to outfits throughout South Texas, including ranches near Laredo, Cotulla, and Eagle Pass, as well as in Frio County. He became foreman of the Halff and Shreiner Ranch when he was twenty and married three years later. In 1927 he became boss of a spread at Sanderson, and in the early 1930s he worked for

Chicago Cattle Loan Company in the Del Rio and Eagle Pass region. He later worked for Raymond Bell on a ranch in Mexico, and ventured to the Alpine area in 1937 to work for Bell's Brown Ranch at Haley Peak (also known as Cathedral Peak). At the age of eighty-seven, he still remembered the dangers of pushing cattle herds across the Rio Grande and Nueces and Leona Rivers. "A horse would go under with an ol' boy and you'd have to throw a rope to him and pull him out," he recalled. Coggins died September 25, 1994, in Alpine.

CONE, CHARLIE. Interviewed 16 October 1990 by telephone, Abilene.

Born May 18, 1905, near Blackwell, Cone began hiring out as a cowboy at age thirteen or fourteen. He cowboyed in the Tatum-Caprock region of eastern New Mexico, as well as for ranches situated near the Texas cities of Seagraves, Lubbock, Levelland, Whiteface, and Muleshoe. In a lot of days out with the wagon, he learned that the cook ruled the roost. "He didn't want anybody to say anything about his food not being good—you didn't ever mention that," he remembered. "If you didn't like it, why, you eat it and said nothing about it, 'cause that's all there was." Cone died in 1992.

DAVIDSON, BILL. Interviewed 22 September 1989, Big Spring.

Born July 7, 1909, in a half-dugout in Stonewall County, Davidson started cowboying at about age twelve. By age thirteen he was breaking horses and doctoring wormy cattle on a ranch near Vincent. In 1929 he signed on with the

Ad Neal outfit at Garden City. "I won't ever forget it—I just had a bedroll and two pair of Levis," said Davidson. He later worked for several other ranches, including the C Bar between Odessa and Monahans, and outfits near Big Lake, Iatan, and Bartlesville, Oklahoma. He went to work for Cosden Oil in 1937, but continued to daywork in his spare time in the Big Spring area until resuming full-time cowboying about 1945. He married in 1948.

DAVIS, ALTON. Interviewed 14 February 1990, Coleman.

Davis was born April 2, 1904, near Utopia and moved at age seven to Junction, where he took up cowboying as a young teenager. He hired on with the Baker Ranch in the Sutton County area in 1925. He cowboyed a dozen or so years on the giant YO (Shreiner) Ranch, which stretched from the Sonora area to near Kerrville, and later worked thirteen years on the Eagle Mountain Ranch near Van Horn. "Back when I growed up and got grown, you'd have dealings with men and you'd shake hands with 'em and that was just good enough," he recalled. "Whenever they told you anything, you could just damn sure depend on it, but you can't do that no more. It's all changed."

DAVIS, L. E. Interviewed 15 February 1990, Tom Green County.

Born July 16, 1899, in Medina County, he lived at an early age on his father's one-section spread near Melvin. In 1910 he helped drive fifty to sixty cows to the Ozona country, where his father had purchased a ranch. After five years in Crockett County, Davis moved with his family to a

175

two-section ranch about fifteen miles northeast of Eldorado. He later hired on with a succession of outfits,
including the Jess Koy Ranch about twenty miles northeast
of Eldorado. "What few of them older men I was around,
wasn't much religious," he recalled of his cowpunching
days. "Of all the damned cussing you ever heard, now they
could really do it." Davis married in 1927.

DAVIS, RALPH. Interviewed 4 March 1989 and 22
July 1989, Sterling City.

The younger brother of Vance Davis, he was born July
12, 1909, in Williamson County and moved to a Sterling
County ranch as a child. He cowboyed for his father as a
youngster, and began hiring out to area ranches at age
twelve. Three years later, he began cowboying full time for
the White and Swearington Ranch in Howard and Glasscock Counties. About 1926, after two stints with the outfit,
he signed on with the U Ranch in Sterling County and soon
became foreman, a position he held until leaving the ranch
in 1942. Davis, who married in 1934, went on to serve sixteen years as a brand inspector for Southwestern Cattle
Raisers Association. "I don't think a young man's ever
done nothing till he's worked on a ranch somewhere," he
observed as he neared eighty. "I think it'd help everybody
to learn to outsmart a cow, outsmart the ol' horse. If I lived
it over, I'd just about do the same."

DAVIS, VANCE. Interviewed 22 September 1989, Big
Spring.

The older brother of Ralph Davis, he was born February 4, 1906, in Runnels County and moved to Sterling

County at an early age. By age twelve he was cowboying regularly. He dayworked for several Howard and Sterling County ranches, including the U Ranch prior to his brother's stay with the outfit. He worked four years in the oil fields before resuming full-time cowboying at Fort Sumner, New Mexico, in 1941. "I stayed with cowboying until I wore out," he said. "I just had to be around them horses." Davis later worked for Sun Oil Company. He died July 5, 1991.

Bill Davidson and Vance Davis in 1989.

DERRICK, FRANK. Interviewed 26 July 1989, Clarendon.

Born December 13, 1913, on the Spur Ranch in the Panhandle, he moved with his family to Clarendon in 1915.

He took up full-time cowboying in the summer of 1931 for W. J. Lewis on the 100-section RO Ranch ten miles northeast of Clarendon. "My father was a cowboy, so I just sort of followed in his footsteps," he said. "I just liked to be out there, to be a-horseback and be around livestock." He also worked on Lewis' 50,000-acre Shoe Bar Ranch, located twenty-five miles south of Clarendon. At the time of the interview, Derrick was still employed by the same ranch company.

DORAN, LEWIS. Interviewed 20 February 1990, Monahans.

Born May 27, 1907, in Menard, Doran moved in 1918 to Concho County, where he learned to cowboy on his father's ranch. "All I wanted to do was run a ranch or be a cowboy; it was in my blood, I guess," he reflected. "I liked the outdoors. It was just my life, working stock." At age twelve, he was a drover for G. Rollie White's Kickapoo Ranch, a 100-section spread between San Angelo and Eden. He worked eight years for the Jim Henderson Ranch in Concho County before signing on with the Jim Callan outfit near Menard in 1928. In 1930 he cowboyed four months in Oklahoma before returning to Texas. In 1938 he ventured to Crockett County, where he cowboyed a total of twenty-four years.

DRENNAN, CHARLIE. Interviewed 26 November 1990, Sterling City.

Drennan was born June 16, 1914, in Scurry County and cowboyed as a youth. His first significant cowboying experience came in 1931, when he hired out to Claude Collins near Stanton. Soon afterward, when Collins transferred him to the 7D Ranch on the Middle Concho River thirty miles south of Sterling City, Drennan first worked sheep. "Them cows, I understood, but I didn't know what to do about them sheep," he recalled. "All I knew was that they went 'Baaaa' and stunk." Nevertheless, Drennan toughed it out, marrying while he was a Collins hand in 1933 and becoming foreman of all the Collins ranches in 1951. He later went into ranching for himself, controlling land at locations such as Mitre Peak in Jeff Davis County and Big Bend Ranch south of Marfa. Drennan died July 14, 1993, in San Angelo.

DUNCAN, TOM. Interviewed 16 October 1990 by telephone, Brady.

Born March 5, 1910, Duncan began cowboying in 1927 on the 45,000-acre Blockhouse Ranch in Mason County. He remained a Blockhouse cowhand for the next eighteen years. Still riding in his late sixties, he suffered a severe injury in a fall. "I was trying to head some calves," he recounted. "My horse stepped in a ditch where there was an oil and gas pipeline. He turned a somerset with me and busted my stomach."

DUNNAHOO, ALPHONZO. Interviewed 18 October 1990 by telephone, Loraine.

Dunnahoo was born November 28, 1901, and began working on ranches in the Loraine area about 1914. In the late 1920s, he cowboyed for the Wimberley Ranch about twelve miles south of Loraine. Stubbornly clinging to the old ways about 1970, he made a sixty-mile cattle drive from

Loraine to the Nine R Ranch west of Snyder. Before ranches practiced dehorning, a cowhand faced added threat, he said. "I've had horned cows and steers hit my horse," he recalled. "I tried to keep 'em from it, but sometimes you couldn't."

DURHAM, WILL. Interviewed 25 February 1989, Sterling County.

Durham was born April 6, 1892, in Iatan and moved with his family to Sterling County when he was two. By the close of the nineteenth century, he already had hired out to the U Ranch on the headwaters of the North Concho River in Sterling County. "Cowboying wasn't an eight-hour proposition, I'll guarantee it," he said. "It was just from you can till you can't." He continued punching cattle for the U outfit until quitting to go to business college at age eighteen or nineteen. Newly married in 1918, he saw service as a U.S. Army soldier in World War I and was a mustard gas victim in Europe. At the time, his prognosis was bleak. "They give me six months to live," he recalled. Nevertheless, he lived another three-quarters of a century, serving as a deputy sheriff and county clerk in Sterling County before dying at age 100 on November 4, 1992.

EDDINS, L. B. "BILL." Interviewed 5 September 1989, Kermit.

Born March 22, 1901, in Palo Pinto County, Eddins moved to a ranch along Sterling Creek in Sterling County in 1904. In 1907 he relocated with his family to a site five miles west of Coyanosa, where his father controlled more than fifty sections astride the Reeves-Pecos county line. He first hired out at age thirteen on the Lake Ranch, a 200-section spread situated southeast of Pecos and owned by Reynolds Cattle Company, or X outfit. When he was about seventeen, he worked for the giant V Staple Ranch in southeastern New Mexico. In December 1918 he signed on with the Sid Kyle spread along the Pecos River in north Loving County and extreme southern New Mexico. Five and a half years later, he went into partnership with his father, only to return to the Kyle Ranch for another stint. He worked in the oil fields in the late 1920s before resuming cowboying on his father's place in 1930. One year later he married. When his father dissolved his cattle herd in 1934, Eddins' cowboying days were over. Still a young man, he went on to serve as a regional cattle inspector in 1935 and 1936 and as Winkler County sheriff from 1947 to 1973. At age eighty-eight, he still had fond memories of punching cattle. "It's a pretty hard life, but it's a good life," he said. "I have no regrets about it. I always liked cattle and horses and usually it was a pretty good bunch of people too." Eddins died March 23, 1991, in Odessa.

FAIRWEATHER, J. E. "JIM." Interviewed 1 March 1989, Midland.

Fairweather was born July 23, 1908, in Panhandle (located 27 miles east of Amarillo) in Carson County. He grew up cowboying on his father's New Mexico ranches: the Shiloh Ranch northwest of Lovington, the nearby Crosby place, and the Maljamar Ranch off the caprock. At the time, much of the Maljamar Ranch was still open range. His memory of the blizzard of January 1918 remained strong even after eight decades. "We had cattle freeze to death," he related. "They drifted to the corner—some of 'em would stay standing up—and their nostrils froze up and they died from a lack of oxygen."

GEORGE, OLAN. Interviewed 1 September 1989, Fort Stockton.

Born May 3, 1908, four miles east of De Leon, George moved with his family to Fort Stockton as a youth. He first hired out in 1924 on the H.D. "Hood" Mendel Ranch west of Fort Stockton. He also cowboyed for the J.T. Baker and Rollie White outfit, the seventy-five- to ninety-five-section Kennedy Ranch west of Fort Stockton, the Charlie Criswell spread, the EL Ranch, and the O8 Ranch north of Fort Stockton. Marrying in 1928, he continued to cowboy on a steady basis for two more years, choosing thereafter to punch cattle seasonally. "I cowboyed in a period of transition," he observed. "Automobiles and mechanized equipment was coming in fast, but that transition was slow in ranching, because people said it would never work, that we'd better go back to teams and horses." Until the 1950s, George engaged in horse-trading. He died April 26, 1992.

GREEN, W. R. Interviewed 9 February 1990, Marathon.

Green was born September 13, 1905, in Colorado City. In 1912 he moved to Brewster County, where his father ranched successively along Maravillas Creek, near McKinney Springs, and at Dugout Wells, five miles east of the Chisos Mountains. He grew up cowboying in what is now Big Bend National Park, attended Sul Ross State Teachers College, and married in his mid-twenties. With a caring cowhand's insight, Green was always a good judge of character. "It's just as simple as can be," he explained. "You can just watch people, and if they're good to their parents and horses, they're good people." Green died in 1992.

GRIFFITH, LONNIE. Interviewed 30 March 1983, Big Spring.

Born in 1904, Griffith moved from Fannin County to Big Spring in 1908. He had been without a father figure since infancy, but soon his mother remarried and they relocated to his stepfather's fifty-three-section ranch on the Colorado River twelve miles south of Gail. "When I was eleven years old," Griffith recalled, "my dad give me a horse and saddle and put me on the payroll at a dollar a day just like the rest of the ranch hands." In the fall of 1918, drouth forced his stepfather to dissolve the ranch and take up an eight-section spread near Luther, where Griffith continued to cowboy for the next few years. "A handshake those days was better than your signature," he noted. "And today, all that you're worth is your signature. The way I was raised, if I told a lie, I got the devil kicked out of me. When a man rode up and asked me something, I told him the truth about it. That was our life then." Marrying in 1926, he took up farming and worked in the oil fields. Later he became a train engineer, serving decades in that capacity. Griffith died March 3, 1984, in Big Spring.

HALL, WEIR. Interviewed 31 October 1990 by telephone, Mertzon.

Born September 30, 1909, in Runnels County, Hall grew up on his father's Runnels County ranch. "I can't remember when I couldn't ride a horse," he noted. He ventured to the Mertzon country about 1927 and worked for several ranches, including the Carlisle outfit on the old Suggs Ranch. He later cowboyed near Barnhart and Big Lake, as well as in Oklahoma.

HENDERSON, THOMAS B. Interviewed 9 February 1990, Marathon.

Born July 4, 1908, in Alpine, Henderson spent his early life on his father's Brewster County spreads: the Pitaya Hill Ranch on Maravillas Creek thirty-three miles south of Marathon, and the Silver Lake Ranch twenty to twenty-five miles downstream near Stillwell Store. "I started doing things when I was seven or eight for my daddy," he remembered. "He didn't mind sending me thirty miles over there horseback with a note stuck in the sweatband of my hat. He sent a note so I wouldn't forget what he told me to tell 'em." In addition to twelve deeded sections of Chihuahuan Desert at Silver Lake, his father controlled another 400 to 500 sections of open range. There on the fringe of present Big Bend National Park, Henderson honed his cowboying skills and punched cattle until 1934, three years after he married. He died July 16, 1990.

HERNANDEZ, LEONARD. Interviewed 29 August 1989, Crane.

Hernandez was born April 11, 1907, near Fort Lancaster in Crockett County. "My dad was a sheepherder and I was born just like a lamb—out in the country," he said. At age eleven, he became a muleskinner, hauling cedar posts and wool in the Spofford area. Within two more years, he was breaking horses. He cowboyed on his step-grandfather's Nueces River ranch until about 1926, when he signed on with the 69 Ranch near Brackettville, his first of several cowboying jobs in the Brackettville-Del Rio area. Returning to Crockett County in 1939, he broke horses for Roy Henderson on the Charco del Caballo Ranch. Hernandez died July 5, 1995, in Camp Wood.

HOELSCHER, WALTER. Interviewed 29 June 1990, Olfen.

Born September 25, 1905, in Olfen, he grew up cowboying on his father's Olfen-area ranches. He and his brother, two years his senior, were his father's only cowhands. Hoelscher participated in his first cattle drive about 1913 and broke his first horse when he was eight. "We were taught that if we started something, we couldn't quit till it was finished," he said. Hoelscher married in 1926 and died May 2, 1996, in Ballinger.

HOOPER, MARVIN. Interviewed 13 November 1989, Crane County.

Born November 27, 1901, in North Dakota, Hooper lived in Virginia as a young child before moving to a 320-acre homestead eight miles north of Tatum, New Mexico, in 1909. About 1917 he took a cowboying job with the 100-section Underwood Ranch twenty-five miles northeast of Tatum. He married in 1928 and continued working for eastern New Mexico outfits until signing on with the Millard Eidson Ranch west of Penwell, Texas, in 1930. Although a cowboy's language was often salty enough to make a sailor blush, Hooper said a hand had to be careful sometimes.

"You didn't cuss anybody out much," he said. "If you did, you'd get hell beat out of you." Hooper died January 8, 1990.

KINSER, L. Interviewed 24 August 1989, San Angelo.

Kinser was born January 25, 1903, in Cleburne and began cowboying about 1926 in King County for SMS Ranches. "I was hungry and needed a job," he recalled. After leaving the SMS in March 1928, he bounced from ranch to ranch before working a year or so for the Triangle outfit near Paducah. He married in the early 1940s and later cowboyed in California. In 1972 he returned to Texas, where, on a Veribest ranch in 1983, he finally climbed off his horse for good at age eighty. He was firm in his conviction that cowboying had given him the best

L. Kinser in 1989.

possible life. "I guarantee you, it was rough," he reflected, "but I liked the freedom and the fresh air and the independence."

LAMBERT, JOE. Interviewed 6 July 1989, Hobbs, New Mexico.

Born June 23, 1899, on a ranch near Rotan, Lambert lived in Fisher County until moving with his family to a half-dugout on a ranch in Dickens County in 1905. "My brother and I were just little bitty kids," he recalled, "but we'd rope a year-old colt and get on him bareback. The ol' colt would throw us, but we couldn't cry and go to the house—we had to get up and get back on him. That's the way I learned to ride broncs." Lambert attended Red Mud School before getting his real education with the SMS, the Half Circle S, the JN Bar, and the Twenty-four outfits. "There's two things I'd like to see back the way it was when I was a kid," he reflected, "and that's the honesty of people and the congeniality of 'em." He quit cowboying in 1919 and spent the next several decades in the oil fields.

LANE, CARL. Interviewed 14 October 1990 by telephone, Robert Lee.

Born May 31, 1908, in Mason County, Lane began to learn the ways of a cowboy at age nine when his father managed a ranch near Goldthwaite. "I started riding on a little ol' horse," he recalled. He began hiring out in 1926, working initially on the Dan Weston Ranch near Knickerbocker. He married in 1930 and signed on with another Knickerbocker outfit for twenty-five dollars a month. He cowboyed for Caton Jacobs at Christoval from 1948 to 1950 and for Claude Collins on the Douthit Ranch at Forsan in the early 1950s. Between ranch jobs, he worked in road construction and in the oil fields. He punched cattle for the last time on the Ray Alderman spread in 1987.

LAUGHLIN, TED W. Interviewed 7 February 1990, Midland County.

Laughlin was born August 13, 1908, in Morgan Mill. At age two he moved with his family to a half-dugout near Elida, New Mexico, where his father had filed a homestead claim. Laughlin first hired out in the summer of 1926 on the giant Littlefield Ranch fifteen miles west of Elida. In September 1927 he signed on with the nineteen-section Paul Horney Ranch north of Clovis, New Mexico, and remained with the outfit until 1935. He then ventured to Arizona, where he cowboyed on a ranch sixty-five miles southeast of Tucson. In 1937 Laughlin returned to Elida and engaged in cattle trading. About 1940 he went to Mexico City as part of a screwworm eradication program. After five years of infantry duty in World War II, he worked briefly for a produce company in Clovis. In 1949, the same year he married, he moved to Glasscock County and hired on with the Wrage Ranch, where he continued to work for the next forty-two years. "We've gone out of the cowboy stage," he reflected at age eighty-one. "There's ropers and bull riders and what-have-you, but when you get right down to it, we've run out of cowboys. Times just change." Laughlin died March 10, 1992, in Midland.

LOEFFLER, S. M. "SI." Interviewed 30 June 1990, Sonora.

Born January 30, 1903, near Mason, Loeffler began helping out on roundups at age twelve on the 20,000-acre Centennial Spring Ranch, a Mason County spread managed by his father. When his father took ill two years later, fourteen-year-old Loeffler hired on steady with the outfit. In the drouth of 1916-1918, he was part of a cattle-skinning operation. When a cow would die, two men would skin the carcass and tie a rope around the hind legs. "My job was to drag 'em off to what they called the bone yard," Loeffler recalled. "There was just dirt, dirt, dirt, and when I'd drag that carcass up there, the dust would fly. I just knew that the world was ruined." In the early 1920s he worked on the Mill Creek Ranch nineteen miles south of Mason. He later entered the banking business.

MANKIN, GREEN. Interviewed 14 September 1989, Mills County.

Mankin was born August 27, 1904, in Mills County and grew up punching cattle. When he was seventeen he rode horseback to Crockett County and hired on with the sprawling Hoover Ranch, one of several area ranches on which he would work. He gained the nickname "Green" through typical cowboy hoorawing. "I met a girl at a rodeo and her name was Clara Green," he remembered. "I'd go to see her, and when somebody would ask where I was, they'd say, 'Oh, he's gone to see Clara Green.' In time they got to calling me Green." He also worked for the Sid Millspaugh outfit, West Pyle Cattle Company near Sanderson, and Rob and Roy Miller in Crockett County. He married in

1931 and left the Ozona country in the Great Depression. He died May 15, 1993, in Mills County.

MAYES, HUDSON "BUD." Interviewed 22 February 1990 and 30 April 1991, Ozona.

Born February 11, 1900, on a farm five miles south of Bronte, Mayes moved with his family to Stiles at age five. By age eight, he was helping his father with ranch chores. He made his first cattle drive at age nine, helping push fifty to seventy-five cow-calf pairs sixty miles from the Jim Lucas Ranch at Stiles to Midland. When he was ten, he moved to a site near present-day Big Lake, where his father had taken a job as foreman of a Ward Cattle Company spread. During World War I, Mayes broke horses for the Blackstone-Slaughter Ranch near Sheffield. After marrying at age twenty-three, he managed a twenty-section ranch that his father had leased just east of Live Oak Creek near Sheffield. He made several cattle drives down the Pecos River in the 1920s and worked on a ranch near Ozona from 1950 to 1964. He cowboyed for the last time at age eighty-two, dayworking west of Ozona. "I just liked ranching and loved horses and cattle and sheep," he reflected at age ninety. "I'd do it all over again." Mayes died December 8, 1996.

McCLELLAN, FRED. Interviewed 6 September 1989, Colorado City.

Born November 4, 1907, in Ledbetter, McClellan moved with his family to West Texas about 1914. He first hired out in September 1925 on the Spade Ranch of Mitchell County, where two of his brothers already worked.

He began as a "flunky," milking cows and hauling firewood, but under the guidance of his brothers, he soon developed into a cowhand. In addition to cowboying on the Spade for several years, he also worked on the Conrad spread in Sterling County. He turned in his spurs for good in 1947, one year before he married. "If you was a good, trustworthy man and could make a hand, you'd usually have a job as long as you wanted it," he reflected. "It was a good life, but I don't know whether I'd want to go over it again." He later took up farming.

Fred McClellan in 1989.

McENTIRE, GEORGE H. JR. "LITTLE GEORGE." Interviewed 15 July 1989, San Angelo.

Born to a pioneer West Texas ranching family on January 14, 1908, in Dallas, McEntire grew up on his father's U Ranch in Sterling County. Although he was familiar with the ranching operation and absorbed much cowboy lore, McEntire admitted he was not much of a cowhand. "Really and truly, I didn't like to ride," he said. "I was not good at riding." An aviator from the age of sixteen, he found his place in the sky and became a test pilot for Lockheed in California in 1941. "At the bottom of the application it asked for any other qualifications I might have," he remembered. "I told 'em I was a pretty good windmill man, I knew how to cook frijole beans, and I'd filled in this application without the aid of an attorney." In eight years with Lockheed, he flew more than 2,000 test flights. He returned to Texas after World War II and remained close to the family ranching operation until his death January 18, 1994, in San Angelo.

MIDKIFF, TYSON. Interviewed 9 August 1989, Rankin; by telephone 11 December 1990, Rankin; and 29 April 1991, Rankin.

Midkiff was born October 22, 1897, in Indian Territory. When he was about three months old, his mother brought him to West Texas, where his father was cowboying on the J Cross in Yoakum County. As an infant, Midkiff lived on a ranch adjacent to Peck Springs, situated southeast of Midland. In 1904 he moved with his family to a site northeast of present-day Midland, where his father homesteaded four sections. By age ten he was cowboying on the spread. As he grew older, he hired out to other outfits, including the NA north of Midkiff, and J.L. Hutt Cattle Company. In 1918 he helped drive a herd of horses to historic Horsehead Crossing on the Pecos. He married in 1922 and later operated ranches in Midland and

Upton Counties, where he continued to fork a horse until suffering a heart attack at age seventy-seven. "I just liked the open range and I liked to ride a horse and work with cattle," he said. Midkiff died May 31, 1991, in Midland.

Tyson Midkiff in 1991.

MURRAH, BUCK. Interviewed 18 October 1990 by telephone, Del Rio.

Born October 22, 1915, Murrah began helping out by age five on his father's ranch along the U.S.-Mexico border west of Sanderson. "You could ride a hundred miles west and east there and not open a gate," Murrah remembered. A third-generation cowboy, he continued to sharpen his skills and was doing a man's job on the spread by age fifteen. During the Great Depression he hired out seasonally to West Pyle Cattle Company and made several cattle drives.

MURRELL, JOHN L. Interviewed 16 October 1990 by telephone, Earth.

Murrell was born September 4, 1910, in Bell County and began cowboying seasonally at age sixteen on the 181,000-acre Mashed O in Bailey and Lamb Counties. In 1929 he took a steady job with the Mashed O and eventually became ranch manager, a position he held until September 15, 1973. During his long decades in the ranching industry, he saw a lot of changes. "I worked for five years for thirty-five dollars a month, and yesterday I paid forty-five dollars for an hour and a half's work," he told the *Lubbock Avalanche-Journal* in 1994.

NORTHCUTT, J. E. "SHORTY." Interviewed 6 September 1989, Spade Ranch, Mitchell County.

Born March 21, 1912, south of Colorado City, Northcutt gained exposure to the cowboying life at an early age. "Our place joined the Spades," he recalled, "and I growed up just sneaking off from school and going to the Spade roundups. I never did learn any book work, but I got a lot of cow savvy." He started as a horse jingler, or wrangler, but soon became a cowhand. At age sixteen he ventured to the Midland country and cowboyed at the Cowden spread northwest of Odessa, the Adobe Ranch near Andrews, the Sand Ranch twenty-five miles southwest of Andrews, and the Tom Nance spread south of Midland. In the early 1930s he broke horses for the Conrad outfit north of Colorado City, then worked on the Spade from 1933 to 1940, during which time he married. After eighteen months with the Scharbauer operation near Midland, he returned to the Spade and eventually became foreman. "I love nature, I love the outdoors," he said in explaining his love for cowboying. "I just don't want to be fenced in." Northcutt died July 20, 1994, in Colorado City.

OWENS, CLAUDE. Interviewed 2 March 1990, Fort Stockton.

Born October 16, 1901, in Ozona, Owens grew up on his father's ranch in west Crockett County. He made his first trail drive at age fifteen, helping push a herd of cattle forty to fifty miles to Big Lake. More drives would ensue. "Our sheep would eat the grass short and the cows would have to be sold," he recalled. His longest drive was one of more than a week from Crockett County to Barnhart. He later

Claude Owens in 1990.

went into ranching for himself, leasing country in the Crockett County region and near McCamey. At the time of the interview, he had a thirty-section spread fifty miles south of Fort Stockton.

PARISHER, TOM WILLIAM. Interviewed 22 February 1990, Ozona.

Parisher was born July 1, 1910, in Cherokee. As a child he lived in southeast New Mexico, Sterling City (from 1914 to 1918), Arkansas, and Callahan County. He took up cowboying in 1928 for the L. Henderson operation at Sheffield. During the next few years he worked for several Sheffield-area ranches, including the Willis Johnson, the Hood Mendel, and the Jeff Harkey outfits. Although Sheffield was only five miles from the Harkey headquarters, Parisher once went eight months without getting into town. "You didn't go to town for fun when you was a-workin'," he noted. Nevertheless, during his 1934 stint with A. C. Noelke on the old Kilpatrick Ranch near Sheffield, he managed to court and marry a school teacher. He also cowboyed on the White and Baker spread east of Fort Stockton.

PATE, JACK. Interviewed 10 March 1990 by telephone, Albany.

Pate was born December 29, 1903, and learned his cowboying skills from his father. At age sixteen he hired out to Reynolds Cattle Company at the 7 Triangles southwest of Albany, then transferred to Reynolds' X Ranch at Kent two years later. In 1926 he left the Kent operation and signed on with the Brite Ranch on the Rio Grande south of

Valentine. After cowboying for a spell in the Sierra Blanca area, he headed north into New Mexico, where he punched cattle for thirty-five years with seldom a spare moment. "Most of us only got off for Christmas and Fourth of July," he noted.

PATTERSON, PAUL. Interviewed 1 April 1983, Crane; 21 June 1989, Castle Gap; 13 November 1989, Hobbs, New Mexico; 2 and 3 March 1990, Alpine; 1 June 1990, Lubbock; 23 June 1990, Castle Gap; 29 April 1991, Crane; and 20 January 1998 by telephone, Pecos.

Born March 28, 1909, on the Brennan Ranch in Gaines County, Patterson cowboyed as a youth for Jake Massingil on King Mountain in Upton County. At about age seventeen, he got his first steady job, punching cattle for John Lane around Upland, King Mountain, and McCamey. Already an experienced hand by his late teens, he rode for Monte Noelke on the 7h outfit in Cedar Canyon south of Rankin before cowboying on the five Arthur Hoover ranches in the late 1920s and early 1930s. He returned to school (eventually earning a degree from Sul Ross State Teachers College) and cowboyed seasonally thereafter, including summers on the Noelke Ranch at Monument Switch near Mertzon and on the McElroy Ranch near Crane. In all, he said, his cowboying experiences added up to "four full years, seven summers, and a thousand weekends." He married in 1939 and went on to teach school for forty years. Gifted with wit and a deft pen, Patterson put his keen insight into the cowboy life to good use and became a beloved Texas folklorist, cowboy poet, humorist, and novelist. "We're the type of people that actually get lonesome for lonesome, if you know what I mean," he said, reflecting on his cowboying days. "When I was baching out here close to King Mountain, I got used to the silence, and I just loved, at night, to hear the bulls coming in to water, you know, and hear the coyotes howling."

POAGE, DOUGLAS. Interviewed 28 September 1990, Ruidoso Downs, New Mexico.

The older brother of Walton Poage, Douglas Poage was born October 12, 1906, in Mertzon. He grew up on a nearby ranch and began cowboying for his grandfather at age twelve. He worked on the J.D. Suggs OH Triangle Ranch near Mertzon in 1922 and on Monte Noelke's 7h Ranch in the spring of 1923. He also cowboyed for the nearby TN and the Sawyer Cattle Company's Bar S before heading to the Midland country in the spring of 1928, working for W.W. Brunson and O.P. Jones, the Clabber Hill outfit, and the Circle Bar. He spent the winter of 1928-1929 on Dick Cowden's H spread west of Midland and the following summer at the Elrod place near Stiles. After another stint with the Circle Bar in the fall of 1929, he worked ten years with a road crew in Reagan County. In the mid-1930s he entered the rodeo arena and became a successful calf roper, competing from New York to Los Angeles and winning a major roping at Albuquerque. In the 1940s he cowboyed in Arizona and welded in the shipyards in Orange. Later, he engaged in ranching. Tall for a cowboy at six feet four inches, he found his size an asset during his cowboying days. "In riding these old crazy horses, you've got the advantage in getting on 'em," he noted. "You're tall and long-legged and you don't have to stretch out to reach so high to get your stirrup and get up there."

POAGE, WALTON. Interviewed 30 August 1989, Rankin.

The younger brother of Douglas Poage, Walton Poage was born August 12, 1908, in Sherwood and grew up on a ranch near Mertzon. He began cowboying for his grandfather at age eleven and first hired out at age thirteen on the Bar S. He worked for the nearby OH Triangles before signing on with the Duane Hughes spread east of Stiles in 1925. When Hughes sold out to Jess Elrod a year later, Poage stayed on with the Elrod outfit for another nine years. He married Elrod's sister in 1935 and entered into a ranching partnership with his brother-in-law. "When you wasn't out with the wagon, you'd just go out and ride and hunt cattle with worms and doctor 'em on the range," he recalled. "If you didn't find any with worms, you'd rope 'em anyway to practice. That's where most cowboys learned to rope." In the mid-1930s he began roping competitively and eventually became a rodeo star, competing throughout the nation and winning the prestigious Madison Square Garden event in New York in 1950 at age forty-two. In the 1940s and 1950s he engaged in numerous match ropings throughout West Texas against fellow cowhand Ted Powers. Poage died December 8, 1995, in Rankin.

POWERS, TED. Interviewed 23 August 1989, San Angelo.

Born February 25, 1907, in the Bull Hollow line camp on the Wylie Ranch near Ballinger, Powers lived in Brown

Green Mankin, Gaston Boykin, and Ted Powers in Comanche in 1983.
(courtesy, Gaston Boykin)

and Runnels Counties as a child. At age sixteen he took up cowboying on the 120-section T Half Circle Ranch in Sutton County. He soon went out to the Ozona country, where he worked for W. R. "Will" Baggett and Walter Babb. "Those Babb boys were the best cowboys I ever saw in my life," noted Powers. "They could ride anything and they could handle wild stock to beat anybody. They had over a hundred sections, and we had to work most of that rough country with a pack horse—you couldn't get through with a wagon." He worked for numerous other Ozona-area outfits, including the Joe Davidson, the Arthur Hoover, the T Half H, and the Sid Millspaugh, as well as for West Pyle Cattle Company at Marathon. After cowboying briefly in Arizona, he returned to Texas and cowboying around Sanderson. He eventually returned to the Davidson Ranch for a seven-year stay. Taking up rodeoing in 1935, Powers became a calf roper of renown, competing from Canada to Mexico and from Florida to California and climbing to third in the world rankings. He married barrel racer Leota Moore in 1941. After retiring from rodeoing, he trained cutting horses and won the world Appaloosa cutting horse title with Mackey's Pride in 1961. Powers died October 31, 1990, in San Angelo.

PROCTOR, LEONARD. Interviewed 2 March 1989, Midland.

Proctor was born September 23, 1892, on a ranch northeast of San Angelo. Moving to his father's five-section ranch forty-five miles southeast of Midland in 1906, young Proctor had a chance to nurture his budding cowboy skills. After marrying in 1921 and punching cattle for several years, he hired on with Texas and Southwestern Cattle Raisers Association as a cattle inspector, a job that lasted thirteen years. He eventually became a leading cattle and sheep rancher, owning or leasing hundreds of thousands of acres. "When the sheep first came in," he noted, "people was kind of prejudiced against them for a while. But they soon found their place." Proctor died August 25, 1994, less than a month shy of his 102nd birthday.

RANKIN, BILLY. Interviewed 9 August 1989 and 29 April 1991, Rankin.

Rankin was born July 9, 1906, in Midland and was reared on his father's ranches in Upton and Midland Counties. By age seven, he already was helping his father cowboy, and at age eight he made his first cattle drive, a twenty-five-mile push from Upton County to Midland. He took up cowboying full-time at age sixteen on his father's forty-one-section ranch in Upton County. In 1924 he broke horses for Foy Proctor, brother of Leonard Proctor. Four years later, Rankin took up an eight-year lease on the forty-one-section Tol Dawson Ranch on the Pecos River near Horsehead Crossing. Reflecting on the character of the typical cowhand, he found only a single shortcoming. "A working cowboy," he observed, "was just like a sheep-herder—he'd save his money, go to town, get drunk, and spend it all. Then he'd borrow a little money to buy him some tobacco and get back to his job." Rankin died August 18, 1995.

REDING, GID. Interviewed 1 September 1989, Fort Stockton.

One of the more intriguing characters ever to fork a horse, Reding was born June 1, 1900, north of Waco and lived as a youth in Ballinger, Arlington, East Texas, Jacksboro, Olney, Arkansas, and Oklahoma. He cowboyed in Colorado before returning to Texas and signing on with an outfit near present Big Lake in 1924. He ventured to the Pecos River region in 1925 and worked for a succession of outfits, including the NH, O-7, Harris Brothers, Blackstone-Slaughter, and Hoover. In 1933 he helped drive a herd of cattle 200 miles from Utah to Flagstaff, Arizona. A year later, he rode horseback from the Mexico border to Montana, where he found ranch work on an Indian reservation. A pioneer aviator, Reding was legendary for his Old West-like brushes with the law and for his unusual ability

Gid Reding in 1989.

with rattlesnakes and broncs. "The main thing about handling animals is you need to get acquainted with 'em," he explained. "With an ol' pony that never saw a man before, you can't go in and rope him, choke him down, and kick him around. Just get in there and crawl around under 'em and pet 'em. They'll find out you ain't gonna kill 'em." Paul Patterson, who shared a line camp with Reding on the Arthur Hoover Ranch near Buena Vista in the winter of 1931-1932, once observed: "Train up a horse in the way Gid Reding sayeth and he will not depart from it." In 1946 Reding finally hung up his spurs and took up farming at Coyanosa. He died March 6, 1993, in Monahans.

REED, MAX. Interviewed 16 October 1990 by telephone, Goldsmith.

Reed was born October 12, 1914, in Mills County, where his father ranched. By age thirteen, Reed had hired out to the Scharbauer Ranch near Midland. In the ensuing years, he spent a lot of time out with the wagon. "Every cook I was ever around was just a little hot-headed," he recalled. "You'd set back, and when he hollered 'Chuck away!,' you went by and just helped yourself [to the food] and got back out of the way. Some of 'em used to holler, 'Come get it 'fore I throw it on the ground!'" He died April 13, 1998, in Wheatridge, Colorado.

RENFRO, WILLARD. Interviewed 14 February 1990, Ballinger.

Born July 22, 1904, in Rochelle, Renfro cowboyed as a teenager for Harold Bevens in Menard, Alvin Neal in McCulloch County, and the Six-Mile Ranch near Fort McKavett. He later punched cattle around Van Horn and Sierra Blanca. Early on, he learned to tolerate the idiosyncrasies of the chuck wagon cook. "We had to kind of go easy on 'em," he said, "'cause, damn, they was about the only ones that cooked anything we could eat."

ROONEY, FRANCIS. Interviewed 14 October 1990 by telephone, Marathon.

Rooney was born October 3, 1899, and grew up in a ranching family. In 1912 he lived at the base of the Chisos Mountains Window, near which his father ranched. He took up cowboying at age thirteen in Brewster County and participated in several trail drives through the Big Bend. Cowboying in those early days, he observed, was "just a rough and tumble job. But that's about all a man had to do then." He married in 1924 and later entered law enforcement, working as a border patrolman and as a peace officer in El Paso before serving twelve years as Presidio County sheriff. Rooney died April 10, 1992.

SHIELDS, BILL. Interviewed 13 October 1990 by telephone, Wellington.

Born December 2, 1899, Shields grew up cowboying with his father. He first hired out at the Wagner Ranch at Vernon in 1917, one year before he married. In 1920 he signed on with the Lee Bivins outfit, for which he worked in Friona and New Mexico. His longest cattle drive was one of more than 200 miles in eastern New Mexico in 1925. He attributed his love of cowboying to a "lack of good sense," considering that the profession offered the "cheapest pay and the hardest and most dangerous work." Nevertheless, he noted, a fellow would "just get it in his system and couldn't get it out." Shields later trained cutting horses.

SMITH, CHARLES KENNETH. Interviewed 12 February 1990, Marfa.

Born October 5, 1894, on the grounds of abandoned Fort Davis, Smith grew up on his father's 25,000-acre Charco de los Marinos Ranch twelve miles north of Marfa. As a boy of seven or eight, he began helping his father cowboy, and by age thirteen he did a man's job as a drover. Three years later he took to neighboring at other ranches. "The cattle weren't as gentle as they are now, because they had run on open range," he recalled. "At first I was just one of the cowboys that did the rough work, mugging the calves down and holding them. Then I got to be the night man. I marked the ears and castrated the bull calves, thousands of them altogether." At the time of the interview, the

Charco de los Marinos was still under his family's control. Smith died March 14, 1990, in Alpine.

SPARKS, ORVAL. Interviewed 14 November 1990 by telephone, San Angelo.

Sparks was born October 8, 1911, and first punched cattle about 1925 on the Benge Ranch in Concho County. Entering into a partnership with a stockman, he ranched and cowboyed in the 1940s in Tom Green County and on twenty sections of the old Spade Ranch in Mitchell County. Although violence was a rarity on the range by the twentieth century, Sparks saw his share. "I've seen two or three murders that still haunt me at times," he said, declining to disclose details in order to spare certain living persons any trauma.

STEVENS, JOHN. Interviewed 13 October 1990 by telephone, Texas Panhandle.

Stevens was born May 3, 1914, and began cowboying, he said, "by the time I could walk." At age seventeen he left home to seek his fortune as a cowhand, but took several years off to get a degree from Texas A&M. Hiring on with the Matador outfit in the Panhandle, he worked his way up to foreman of the Alamositas Division in 1940. Six years later he became Matador Division manager.

STOKES, AUBREY. Interviewed 13 October 1990 by telephone, Vealmoor.

Born August 1, 1907, Stokes began cowboying as a youth of eight or so in Scurry County. He later went on several cattle drives, including one of 200 miles that originated in King County in 1926. He also cowboyed on the John B. Slaughter operation west of Post. With a cowhand having little time for social affairs, Stokes was introduced to his future wife in classic cowboy fashion. "I met her," he said, "in a cow trail at Gail."

STROUP, J. R. "JIM." Interviewed 27 July 1989, Quitaque.

Born August 3, 1903, in Briscoe County, Stroup was reared on the Rocker X, his father's Briscoe County ranch. "My mother said she thought I was born with boots on," Stroup related. "I started riding awfully early in life. When I was six and seven years old, I'd trail along behind my father for half a day at a time out in the breaks." As he grew toward manhood, Stroup continued to cowboy on the spread, which ranged in size from fourteen to twenty-two sections. While attending college, he purchased a section of land, the start of a long-term ranching enterprise. Looking back on his cowboying years, he noted that it took a special breed to be an effective cowhand. "There's a lot of people who are just like a horse," he observed. "There's a lot of horses that you can't make cow horses out of; there's a lot of men that never learned how to work cattle."

TAYLOR, TROY "JONES." Interviewed 26 July 1989, Silverton.

Jones was born March 1, 1912, and grew up on his family's ranch in Floyd and Briscoe Counties. He developed cowhand skills at an early age and applied his know-how to the family operation as an adult. "We worked seven days a week most of the time," he recalled. Even so, he had no regrets, noting that punching cattle "just kinda gets in your blood."

TOWNSEND, BILL. Interviewed 22 July 1995 by telephone, Vera; 3 August 1995, Odessa.

Born February 8, 1906, Townsend grew up in Fluvanna and got his first horse-breaking job in 1923 in Borden County. In the mid-1920s he worked for the Slaughter operation near Post, the Matadors, and the Beal outfit near Gail. After driving a horse herd from Fluvanna to Ozona in August 1928, he stayed in Crockett County and punched cattle for several years, working for Arthur Hoover, Joe Davidson, Jordan Montgomery, Burt Couch, Sid Millspaugh, and others. He also cowboyed near Buena Vista and Pyote. After leaving the Pecos River country, he managed a ranch near Albany from 1934 to 1941. He married thereafter, purchased a small stock farm, and gave up cowboying. He was still in his thirties, but the strenuous job of punching cattle was a young man's profession. "I remember hearing back then that a cowboy's life was twelve years on the average—they either quit or something happened," he noted. "What they call the 'cowboy life' was working for somebody else, you know. Some of them boys would get a little stuff of his own and quit, move out on his own. He'd still work cattle, but his cowboy life was over."

VILLALBA, CHON. Interviewed 9 February 1990, Fort Stockton.

Villalba was born March 25, 1900, on a Pecos County ranch and longed to be a cowhand even as a child. "I remember when I went to school, 1909, 1910, the teacher asked me what I'd like to be," he recounted. "I told her right quick, 'A cowboy.' It just come natural." He was fifteen when he landed his first riding job, hiring on with Morgan Livingston's Pecos River outfit northeast of Fort Stockton. He also worked for the 8-0 Ranch east of Fort Stockton, Scharbauer Cattle Company, the Shell Ranch near Sanderson, Sam White and Lloyd White, Hood Mendel west of Fort Stockton, Hence Barrow near Odessa, and Fred Harrell southeast of Fort Stockton. He last cowboyed in 1964 at the age of sixty-four. Villalba died May 15, 1992, in Fort Stockton.

VINES, P. O. "SLIM." Interviewed 16 August 1989, Crane.

Born June 11, 1909, Vines grew up on farms in Ellis County and Colorado City. From 1924 to 1927 he dayworked for Henry Hammonds and the Spade Ranch in Mitchell County. At age eighteen in 1927, he hired on with the sixty-section O.P. Jones Ranch, or Open A outfit, thirty-five miles south of Midland. Carrying only 120 pounds on his six-foot, one-inch frame as a young man, Vines soon gained the nickname "Slim." In the early 1930s he cowboyed for Fred Snyder, the Murray outfit north of Rankin, W. W. "Billy" Brunson on the L7 Ranch, and the McElroy Ranch near Crane. He made numerous cattle drives, including one of eighty-five-days' duration from south of Midland to Whiteface in the fall of 1930. In 1935 Vines went to work for Gulf Oil Company, but continued to daywork in his spare time. From the vantage point of eighty years of life in 1990, he had no trouble understanding his early passion for punching cattle. "When you're young like that," he explained, "you're looking for excitement, and there was always a bunch of excitement around cattle and horses."

WHATLEY, WOOD. Interviewed 10 March 1990 by telephone, Quanah.

Born January 20, 1901, in Anson, Whatley started out cowboying as a kid near Tucumcari, New Mexico. At age seventeen he worked southwest of Childress on the CV Ranch, a Matador spread. He also cowboyed for the Tabor outfit on the Pease River south of Quanah. Venturing to Colorado, he spent ten and a half years managing three ranches. "I've had horses that fell on me, bucked me off, horses that pawed me, horses that kicked me," he said. "Everybody always said if I ever died, they'd know a horse killed me."

WILSON, MAYNARD "FISH." Interviewed 27 July 1989, Quitaque.

Born February 21, 1908, in Arkansas, Wilson moved to Briscoe County in 1915. He started out "water-gapping" on the Jackson Collier spread east of Quitaque at age seventeen. He soon graduated to cowboying, working for a succession of area outfits, including Burson Cattle Company and Sam Bell. He gained his unusual nickname while attending school in Quitaque about 1919. "There was a boy in my grade who couldn't say my name, 'Maynard,'" he recounted. "He called it 'Mynard'—he couldn't put that 'A' in it. The teacher couldn't understand who he meant, and he said, 'Well, minnow fish.' They dropped the minnow and just used 'fish.' All the cowboys at the JA's never did know what my name was; I was just 'Fish Wilson.'" The JA Ranch, with which he signed on in 1940, held its cowboys to the same high standards that co-founder Charles Goodnight established in the 1800s. "You was fired at the JA's for three things," Wilson remembered, "and that was for drinking and fighting and gambling." In addition to punching cattle, Wilson farmed and served five years as a brand inspector for Texas and Southwestern Cattle Raisers Association.

WITT, JIM. Interviewed 17 July 1993 and 22 July 1995 by telephone, Loving, New Mexico.

Born November 3, 1914, he moved with his mother to the Cross C Ranch on the Pecos River near Barstow at the age of nine. He grew up on the spread and learned the ways of a Pecos cowboy. "It was hard work, just a lot of hard work," he recalled. "If course, you did everything on horse, and you didn't haul your horse down to somewhere and unload him—you rode him down there. But it was interesting work and I loved it." Witt stayed on with the Cross C until 1933 or 1934, when he went to work for Safeway in nearby Pecos for fifteen dollars a week, twice the pay of a cowhand. But even as he worked his way up to store manager (one of the youngest in the Safeway chain), he continued to daywork as a cowboy.

YEARY, FRANK. Interviewed 26 July 1989, Silverton.

Yeary was born November 3, 1909, in Floyd County, where he cut his cowboy teeth at age twelve or thirteen for the Lewis and Letts operation. After ten years with the outfit, he hired on with a succession of sprawling ranches in the Panhandle—the Matador, the Pitchfork, the SMS, the Four Sixes. He cowboyed for a spell in Arizona and signed on with the Figure Five near Forsan in the 1940s. Like many cowboys, he married late, waiting until he was forty-two. A couple of years later in 1954, he finally turned his horse out to pasture and took up farming. Cowboying was a rough life, he said, but he would have had it no other way. "When I was forty years old, I was older than I ought to have been at sixty," he noted. "I'd lived like a coyote in some ol' camp, and I'd been kicked and run over and beat up. But I enjoyed ever' minute of it."

YOUNG, SETH. Interviewed 23 February 1990 by telephone, Uvalde.

Born September 12, 1902, near Rocksprings, Young started riding when he was only four on his father's 2,500-acre ranch in Edwards County. He went on his first cattle drive as a boy of eight about 1910. "We slept out on a pallet that night, first night I ever slept out in my life," recounted Young. "I'd see the stars fall, and I asked my daddy, 'How long will it take all these stars to fall?'" At age twelve, Young began dayworking in the Hill Country, and two years later he graduated to the role of a full-fledged drover. He married in 1923, taught school for a while, then entered the ranching business. At age eighty-seven, he reflected on his life in the saddle. "I was born wanting to ride," he said simply.

Index

Olfen, 43, 84
Owens, Claude, 44, 149, 195
Ozona, 36, 58, 123, 137, 141, 147, 149

P

Paducah, 33
Palo Duro Canyon, 5-7, 161
Parisher, Tom William, 18, 21-22, 196
Park Springs Ranch, 46
Pate, Jack, 36-37, 123, 156, 196-197
Patterson, Paul, 8, 15, 19, 119, 197-198
Paul Horney Ranch, 45
Pecos, 61
Pecos River, 18, 27, 32, 90
Penwell, 142, 144
Poage, Douglas, 28, 58-60, 123, 131-132, 198-199
Poage, Walter, 152
Poage, Walton, 153, 199
Pool Ranch, 128, 152
Powell, Ead, 33
Powers, Ted, 15, 46, 58, 72, 76, 116, 118, 138, 146, 199-200
Powers, Tom, 137-139
pranks, 116-132, 143, 147-150, 155
    at camp, 151-153
    horses pitching, 121-127, 129-131
    ill-advised, 154
    on greenhorns, 116-121, 146-150
    paybacks, 155-160
Proctor, Leonard, 75, 101, 201

Q

Quien Sabe Ranch, 115-116

R

rain,
    predicting, 12, 15
    storms, 15-17, 19, 21-24, 32-34

working in, 31-34, 90, 102, 110-111
Rankin, 77
Rankin, Billy, 116, 140, 201-202
Reagan County, 88
Red River, 5, 7
Reding, Gid, 54, 76, 202-203
Reed, Max, 16, 31, 46, 116, 203-204
Renfro, Willard, 48-49, 64-65, 87, 103-104, 155-156, 204
Reynolds Creek, 50
Rio Grande, 114
Rocksprings, 32, 104
Rogers, Will, 141
Rooney, Francis, 78-79, 204-205
Rotan, 22

S

San Angelo, 101
San Antonio, 149
San Saba River, 106
Sand Windmill, 144
sandstorms, 11
Sangre de Cristo Mountains, 37
Scharbauer, 46
Scharbauer Cattle Company, 31, 100
Schleicher County, 122
screwworms, 38
sheep, 19
Sheffield, 90
Sheppard, Roy, 126
Shields, Bill, 12, 25, 52, 94, 205
Silver Lake, 50
Silver Lake Ranch, 63
Six-Mile Ranch, 155
Slaughter, Oran, 155
Smith, Charles Kenneth, 49, 205-206
Smith, Tyrrel, 49
SMS Ranch, 33, 159
snow, working in, 34-37

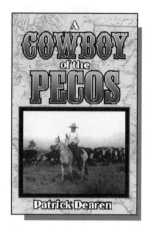

A Cowboy of the Pecos

Patrick Dearen

An 1886 newspaper termed the Pecos River of Texas and southern New Mexico "the cowboy's paradise." One cowhand even reckoned "the Pecos boys were the most expert cowboys in the world." On the Pecos they had to be, for in frontier times it was a river so treacherous it was known as the "graveyard of the cowman's hopes."

This account tells the full story of the Pecos cowboy, from the time of the Goodnight-Loving cattle drive to the 1920s. Documented and supported by vintage photographs, this book will carry readers through the Old West with the cowboys.

240 pages • 5½ x 8½ • softbound
1-55622-528-8 • $12.95 US

Other Books

Alamo Movies
At Least 1836 Things You Ought to Know About Texas But Probably Don't
Battlefields of Texas
Best Tales of Texas Ghosts
Bubba Speak
Critter Chronicles
Daughter of Fortune: The Bettie Brown Story
Defense of a Legend
Etta Place: Her Life and Times with Butch Cassidy and the Sundance Kid
Exploring Dallas with Children
Exploring San Antonio with Children
Exploring Texas with Children
Exploring the Alamo Legends
Eyewitness to the Alamo
First in the Lone Star State
Fixin' to Be Texan
Funny Side of Texas
Ghosts Along the Texas Coast
Great Texas Airship Mystery
Horses and Horse Sense
Letters Home: A Soldier's Legacy

Phantoms of the Plains
Rainy Days in Texas Funbook
Red River Women
Return of Assassin John Wilkes Booth
Return of the Outlaw Billy the Kid
Spindletop Unwound
Spirits of San Antonio and South Texas
Tales of the Guadalupe Mountains
The Texas Golf Guide
Texas Highway Humor
Texas Politics in My Rearview Mirror
Texas Ranger Tales
Texas Ranger Tales II
Texas Tales Your Teacher Never Told You
Texas Wit and Wisdom
That Cat Won't Flush
They Don't Have to Die
This Dog'll Hunt
To the Tyrants Never Yield
Trail Rider's Guide to Texas
Treasury of Texas Trivia
Unsolved Mysteries of the Old West
Unsolved Texas Mysteries
When Darkness Falls

Call us at **972 / 423-0090** or visit our web site at **www.wordware.com**.